color book

The Aura-Soma pomander oils included in this kit contain the following ingredients:

Original White Alcohol Denatured, Aqua (Water), *Pelargonium graveolens* (Rose Geranium) flower oil, *Calendula officinalis* (Calendula) flower extract, *Melaleuca alternifolia* (Tea Tree) leaf oil, *Arnica montana* (Arnica) flower extract, *Cupressus sempervirens* (Cypress) oil, *Gaultheria procumbens* (Wintergreen) leaf oil, *Lavandula angustifolia* (Lavender) flower oil, *Pimenta acris* (Bay) leaf oil, *Rosmarinus officinalis* (Rosemary) leaf oil, *Citrus aurantium bergamia* (Bergamot) fruit oil, Menthol

Red Alcohol Denatured, Aqua (Water), *Cedrus atlantica* (Cedarwood) bark oil, *Pimenta acris* (Bay) leaf oil, Menthol, *Santalum album* (Sandalwood) oil, *Eugenia caryophyllus* (Clove) flower oil, Parfum (fragrance), CI 15510, CI 17200, CI 19140

Orange Alcohol Denatured, Aqua (Water), *Santalum album* (Sandalwood) oil, *Citrus aurantium bergamia* (Bergamot) fruit oil, *Citrus aurantium amara* (Bitter Orange) peel oil, *Citrus nobilis* (Mandarin orange) peel oil, CI 15510, CI 17200

Yellow Alcohol Denatured, Aqua (Water), *Verbena officinalis* (Verbena) oil, *Cymbopogon nardus* (Citronella) oil, *Cymbopogon schoenanthus* (Lemongrass) oil, CI 15510, CI 19140

Emerald Green Alcohol Denatured, Aqua (Water), *Citrus aurantium bergamia* (Bergamot) fruit oil, *Rosmarinus officinalis* (Rosemary) leaf oil, Menthol, *Melia azadirachta* (Neem) leaf extract, *Melia azadirachta* (Neem) flower extract

Royal Blue Alcohol Denatured, Aqua (Water), *Commiphora myrrha* (Myrrh) resin, *Mentha piperita* (Peppermint) oil, Parfum (fragrance), Menthol, CI 42090, CI 60730

Violet Alcohol Denatured, Aqua (Water), *Commiphora myrrha* (Myrrh) resin, *Eucalyptus globulus* (Eucalyptus) leaf oil, Parfum (fragrance), CI 60730, CI 17200

color book

use the healing power of
color to transform your life

Lori Reid

special photography by Claire Paxton

CONNECTIONS
BOOK PUBLISHING

To Lisa Eveleigh—a ray of sunshine

A CONNECTIONS EDITION
First published in Great Britain in 2000 by
Connections Book Publishing Limited
St Chad's House, 148 King's Cross Road
London WC1X 9DH

This edition published in U.S.A. in 2001 by
Connections Book Publishing Limited
Distributed in U.S.A. by Samuel Weiser, Inc.
Weiser Books, P.O. Box 612
York Beach, ME 03910-0612

British Library Cataloguing-in-Publication data available on request.

ISBN 1-85906-044-7

10 9 8 7 6 5 4 3 2

Phototypeset in Sabon MT and Swiss 721 BT using QuarkXPress on Apple Macintosh.
Origination by Bright Arts, Singapore.
Produced in China by Leo Paper Products Ltd.

Contents

Introduction

Color can influence our moods and feelings

From the first flush of palest rose at dawn to the deeper shades of violet and magenta at sunset, our days are filled with the vibrancy of a million colors. When the sun shines, colors come alive, our hearts fill with joy, and life feels good. The sky is azure, the grass is jewel green, and the oceans scintillate the deepest jade. It seems we cannot help but respond to the colors that make up our world.

In Nature, color alternates with the seasons to create an ever-changing canvas that excites the eye and soothes the soul.

Color and emotion

Psychologists studying the effects of light have discovered that color can influence our bodies, moods, and feelings. Red, the color of fire and passion, has the power to excite the senses. Blue, cooling and quietening, brings serenity, calms our feelings, and slows our reactions.

Sit in a red room and your chatter will become animated and time will fly by. Sit in a blue room and your thoughts will become introspective. Relax, there is no need to hurry. Time will hang heavier here. Each color has its own properties and exerts its individual influence, subtly impacting on our emotions and behavior in different ways. Green brings us solace, orange, joy, and violet inspiration.

It is only by becoming aware of these effects that we can harness the power of color and actively use it to express our feelings or to change key aspects of our lives. Create a completely new atmosphere in your home by simply changing the décor. Improve your image by wearing the colors that bring your face alive. Or even enhance your health by focusing on the colors that will help to bring balance and harmony to your body and mind.

Energy and healing

Besides bringing brightness into our lives, color is a dynamic energy in its own right and has been used as a therapeutic tool for thousands of years. Evidence suggests that color healing and light therapy reached very high levels of efficacy in ancient Egypt during the reign of the pharaohs. Happily, as we begin the third millennium, we are beginning to see a revival of interest, with new applications being developed all the time for this magical and non-intrusive type of therapy.

Learn to use color to express your feelings, as a mirror to understand your deepest motivations, and as a special tool to help bring happiness and beauty into your life.

Seeing color

To see a color is such a complex business that the whole process could be described as magical. Color is not a pigment. It is not tangible, nor is there anything solid about it. Essentially, a color is a frequency, carried in wave form, just like heat or sound. It is a component of light that is radiated by the sun and, as such, is a form of energy in its own right. Like individual notes of music, each color vibrates along its own specific wavelength—change the frequency and you change the color.

So, if a color is a vibration, how then can it be seen? And how, for that matter, can we distinguish red from green, or blue from yellow? To put it simply, the process of seeing a color all takes place in the brain.

The science of color

As light streams out from the sun, it carries with it the different frequencies by which colors are transmitted. These frequencies can be separated by a process known as refraction, which was first demonstrated at the end of the seventeenth century by Isaac Newton, the great British physicist.

Newton showed that when a beam of light is passed through a prism it divides into the seven color rays, called the spectrum. Rainbows are formed by the same process of refraction when rays of sunlight, striking water droplets in the atmosphere, are broken up into their component colors. The larger the droplets, the brighter the rainbow will appear in the sky. We can appreciate Newton's discovery every time we see light shining through a faceted glass pendant or a crystal chandelier.

How we perceive color

Objects do not possess inherent colors of their own. When we see a yellow banana or a red rose, it does not mean that, in reality, the banana is colored yellow or the rose red. It simply means we perceive them as those colors—because our brains tell us so.

What we actually think we see as the pigment of an object is, in fact, the color that the object is reflecting away from itself. When a ray of sunlight hits a banana, the fruit absorbs all the rays of the spectrum except yellow. Because it is the yellow ray that the banana reflects, this is the color that is thrown back to our eyes and which we pick up. Strange as it may seem, the very color that we associate with the banana is the one that it rejects.

In just the same way, a rose absorbs all the colors except red, a blade of grass rejects green, and a goldfish throws off orange.

Inside the eye

Our eyes are specially adapted to receive messages about light and color, which they transmit to the brain for decoding. When the banana throws off the yellow, its frequency enters the lens of the eye and is directed to special receptors in the retina called rods and cones. These receptors collect the information and send it through the optic nerve to the brain. Here, the particular characteristics of the

Light passing through a prism is refracted and broken into the colors of the rainbow. If the separate colors are passed back through another prism, they will re-form as white light.

incoming frequencies are interpreted to determine the color.

There are around 7 million cones in the human eye, and it has been estimated that we have the capacity to pick out and differentiate between approximately 10 million different shades of color. When you consider how many colors you take in with the merest glance across a room, you will appreciate what a feat for the brain color recognition must be!

Individual wavelengths

Of the seven colors in the spectrum, violet has the shortest wavelength. Beyond that is ultraviolet, a powerful ray that can pass through the body unseen and has the capacity to kill bacteria and tan our skin. At the other end of the spectrum lies red, with the longest wavelength. Beyond this is infrared, the heat-seeking ray that can light up a body in the black of night. Microwaves, radar, radio, and television frequencies, all invisible, are found still farther along this continuum. But it is only that part of the spectrum from red to violet, with the intervening colors orange, yellow, green, blue, and indigo, that is visible to the naked eye.

The growth of perception

Scientists believe that primitive humans were capable of perceiving very few colors, and that only through evolution has it been possible to see the full range that is now available to us. Could it be, then, that there are still more colors in the spectrum? Colors that we are unable to perceive because we have not evolved the capacity to see them?

Besides demonstrating the properties of light, Isaac Newton also created the color wheel, a clever device showing how colors are related to each other. These are described on page 11.

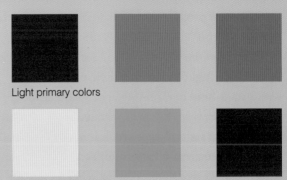

Light primary colors

Light secondary colors

Color and light

There is a difference between the colors of light and the colors in pigments, which are used in paint. Newton discovered three pure colors in light—red, blue and green. When mixed together, these make the three secondary colors of yellow, cyan, and magenta. Combining the six produces white light. Different from the primary colors of light, the three primary colors in paint are red, blue and yellow (see pages 10–11).

animal vision

Research into the color vision of animals suggests that only the higher primates have the ability to see the full spectrum of colors. Other species may have the capacity to see two or three colors at most, but it is thought that animals are, in the main, color–blind. These findings, then, would give a lie to the belief that the color red enrages a bull!

Color kinships

Solid colors containing pigment, such as those used in paints or fabrics, combine differently from light color. The primary colors here are red, yellow, and blue. These combine to make secondary colors. Combining a primary with its neighboring secondary colors takes us to another level—of tertiary colors.

These relationships are clearly seen when arranged in a color wheel (right). Here, the three primaries are equidistant from one another. The secondaries are inserted inbetween, following the sequence of a rainbow. The resulting six tertiaries are slotted in, each one between a primary and a secondary. Use the color wheel to make decisions on color schemes in your home or when choosing clothes.

Changing hues

We can continue the process of mixing adjacent pairs together to form even more colors, but literally thousands of new variations can be produced by the addition of black or white. Mixing black into any color in the wheel makes the original color darker, creating a shade. When white is added to make the base color lighter, the result is known as a tint or a tone. Gray can be added to achieve a muted effect.

Gauging the temperature

Colors may also be described as warm or cool. Red, which we associate with fire; orange with burning coals; and yellow; with sunshine, are warm colors. They are carried on longer wavelengths, so they are perceived as dominant, or advancing colors, reaching the eye faster than the colors in the other half of the spectrum.

Greens, blues, and violets, on the other hand, are experienced as cool colors and bring to mind the waters of the ocean, the dew-soaked grass at dawn, or bluebells carpeting a shady grove. Because these are carried on a shorter frequency, their light takes longer to reach the eye and are therefore described as receding.

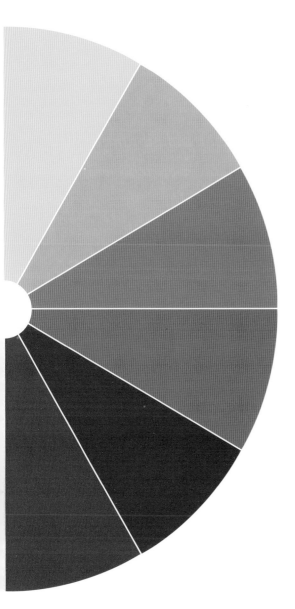

The color wheel

Seeing the colors arranged in a color wheel is extremely useful in helping us to understand the relationships between colors and how they work with each other. A color wheel can prove an invaluable tool when choosing colors for interior decorating, for example, or for matching a new outfit to an existing wardrobe.

primary colors

Red, blue, and yellow are primary, or foundation, colors. They cannot be created by mixing other colors.

secondary colors

By mixing two primary colors, we can create secondary colors. So, the combination of red and yellow gives us orange, yellow and blue make green, and blue and red makes violet.

tertiary colors

Combining a primary with its neighboring secondary color creates a tertiary color. Turquoise, for example, is made in this way, by mixing primary blue with secondary green.

complementary colors

Colors opposite each other on the wheel are known as contrasting or complementary. Used together in their purest forms, these colors will clash. However, complementary colors can produce an interesting, and much less jarring, visual effect when muted and used as tints.

related colors

Two colors adjacent to one another on the color wheel have a common base and are, therefore, called harmonious, or related, colors. Related colors work well together and do not jar the eye. Using related or harmonious colors in a room scheme can produce a very pleasing effect.

Part One

The psychology of color

Glorious color
enriches every
aspect of
our lives

Color is glorious. Vivid and vibrant or muted and mellow, colors enrich our lives. But to fully appreciate color is to recognize its extraordinary powers. For color exerts a subtle yet potent influence that affects us all. Try as we might, we cannot avoid responding to the different colors around us. They affect our moods, mirror our emotions, change our behavior, and even alter the way we look.

Becoming aware of the effects of color means that we can make use of its positive benefits to lift our spirits, to unlock our creative imagination, to enhance our environment, and to improve our image, our well-being, and our lives.

Introducing color psychology

Everyone has a different perception of color

We all perceive colors differently. The green I see may not be exactly the same shade or tone as the green you see—even though we may be looking at the same blade of grass at the same time.

In part, this is due to our individual physiological makeup, the way our bodies respond to the light that enters through our eyes and stimulates the pituitary gland (the master gland that controls our hormones). But to a large extent, too, our perception of color is shaped by our own personal thoughts and memories. When a color becomes associated with a particular experience, it will thereafter remind us of that event.

Color and memory

Remember the first time you fell in love—how all your senses were heightened, how vivid the sky seemed, how bright the flowers? The color of the outfit you were wearing that day, or the particular shade of the shirt on your lover's back, may now be indelibly imprinted in your subconscious and will forever be associated in your mind with rapturous joy. Now consider a very different scenario—one of being attacked or assaulted. Imagine how the very same shade that conjures up euphoria for you, might convey only terror to someone whose attacker had worn that very color. Both memories are no less powerful than each other, both contain visions of the same color, but the associations attached to that color will differ markedly from one to the other and, moreover, from then on will influence how that color is experienced.

Color, then, is all to do with perception. You could say, it is in the eye of the beholder.

The dulled colors of a cloudy day have a lowering effect on our spirits. Contrast this to the joyous feelings we experience when the sun shines out from a bright blue sky.

The power of color

Color is a powerful tool. It acts on our bodies, minds, and emotions, triggering deep and subtle responses on a subconscious level. Try as we might, we simply cannot avoid reacting to color. On dark, overcast days, when the light is poor and the colors in our environment are dulled, we feel miserable and low in energy. How different we feel on a sunny day, when colors are vibrant, lifting our mood and bringing us optimism and a blitheness of heart.

Studies have shown that different colors exert different physiological effects. Red, orange and yellow have an invigorating action on the body. They pump up our blood pressure, stimulate our pulse, and increase our breathing rate. These hot colors come across essentially as tonics which vitalize and shake us awake.

Acting as a fulcrum, green lies at the center of the scale, balancing and reconciling the disparate properties of the "hot" colors with those of the "cold" colors at the other end of the spectrum. Here lie blue, indigo, and violet—cooler shades which soothe and bring us tranquilizing balm at the end of a hectic day.

Sit under a red light for too long and you are likely to get restless and develop a headache. Switch to a blue light, and you will soon cool down and feel quite calm again.

Because colors stimulate the nervous system in their own individual ways, they can even affect a person's perception of passing time. For example, an hour appears to fly past when spent in a red room, whereas the same hour in a room painted a restful shade of green seems to stretch out far beyond its actual sixty minutes.

Personality testing

Because of color's different frequencies, each color has very individual properties. As we know, red can invigorate while blue can tranquilize. Orange can make us feel buoyant, and indigo has the potential to send us into a philosophical contemplation. A person who likes a quiet life may find the excitable effects of red quite disturbing. Similarly, a lively youngster could find his exuberant spirit stultified by the sobering influences of navy.

We all have colors that we love and others that we detest. What can these tastes tell us about ourselves? Psychologists have explored this inclination and have come to realize that colors can be used to throw light on our characters, our emotions, our preferences, and our behavior in life (see page 16–17).

color speaks

In times past, color was described as "the language of the soul". Indeed, through color we can express many emotions.

black for sorrow

red for passion

green for envy

white for peace

Psychological research

> Color has
> a powerful
> effect on our
> behavior and
> emotions

The psychological effects of colors have attracted a good deal of interest in the scientific world, and studies have confirmed that colors do indeed influence us in many subtle ways.

Researchers working with children, for example, have found that the décor in the classroom has an important influence on learning ability and IQ rates. A brown or black environment seems to be particularly detrimental, significantly reducing the rate at which children absorb information. Brightly painted classrooms, on the other hand, have a positive effect on the IQ of their young occupants. Yellows and oranges proved the most effective and, when painted around the chalkboard, noticeably improved both learning and attention.

Cars, colors, and character

Even when it comes to buying cars, color is important in the choices we make. Researchers have shown that there is a definite link between personality, behavior, and the color of the vehicle we choose to drive.

When able to choose, high achievers were found to go for cars in neutral shades, and those who are less competitive drove brightly colored cars. Studies also revealed that a greater percentage of neutral-colored vehicles tend to be involved in speeding offenses, reflecting precisely what we might expect from their high-achieving owners, with their dynamic and competitive tendencies. Another observation showed that the more expensive the make of car, the more conservative its color was likely to be. This suggests that car manufacturers have carefully considered their market and discovered that individuals who can afford to buy vehicles at the top end of the price range prefer sober shades, whereas cheaper models sell well in brighter colors.

neutral shades

Neutral or sober shades like beige, gray, charcoal, and maroon are often chosen by high-achieving professionals, who can be competitive drivers.

bright colors

Red, blue, yellow, and other brightly colored cars are often driven by people who are less interested in success and material gain.

In the pink

In the 1980s, studies were carried out to determine what effect color has on aggression. Cells in correctional centers in the United States were painted in various colors from white to red, and prisoners allocated to each of the cells were monitored both for their physiological responses and for their behavior. The findings were interesting and revealed that prisoners in the cells that were painted a particular shade of pink were significantly less abusive and violent than those in cells of any other color. The shade of pink is quite specific and is known as "Baker-Miller pink." It is now widely used in both police cells and psychiatric wards, where it has been found to successfully reduce arousal and calm the emotions of particularly volatile inmates.

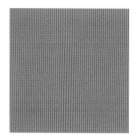

The psychology of winning

Color has been found to have an effect on the results of team sports such as hockey and football. American researchers, studying the results of football and hockey games, found that teams who wear a black strip are more likely to have penalties awarded against them than teams wearing uniforms in any other color.

Teams who wear white tend to be penalized the least, and red, a popular color in sport, gives a dynamic appearance to the team, imbuing its wearers with energy, vigor, and dash.

Sporting colors

The idea that the color of our clothes can influence both us as the wearer and those with whom we come into contact, is nowhere more evident, it seems, than on the playing field.

Three possible explanations were put forward by psychologists who found that teams wearing black were penalized more than those wearing any other color. Players wear black to convey a mean and intimidating image which "psychs" them up to win. The second possible interpretation is that wearing black does actually have an aggressive effect on the players. Thirdly, black is seen as aggressive from the outset, so the referee may subconsciously be predisposed to treat them as spontaneous aggressors. As a consequence, a misdemeanor on the field will be perceived as their fault and a penalty more likely to be awarded against them.

In light of this data, the old preconception that heroes wear white and villains wear black springs to mind.

What our favorite colors say about us

Have you ever stopped to think why you like one particular color more than any other? What is it about your favorite color that makes it your favorite? Is it because it inspires you, makes you feel good when you look at it or makes you look great when you wear it? Has it been your favorite since childhood, or have you changed your mind several times in your life? It is not until we start to ask ourselves questions of this kind that we discover quite how fascinating our reasons are.

Memories and images

Close your eyes and think about your favorite color. What images does it bring to your mind? What feelings and emotions does it evoke in your soul? And what situations does it conjure up? Now try it again with a color you positively dislike. Think of the color and ask yourself how it makes you feel. Then ask yourself why you might be responding in that way. What is it you associate with this color: revulsion; unhappiness; discomfort; fear?

Apart from the fact that we're turned on or off colors by what we associate them with—blood and feces are common alienators—there are several other theories to explain why we like and dislike certain colors.

One suggestion has to do with vibrations. We know scientifically that each color has its own frequency, and we believe, too, that our bodies, organs, and thoughts produce electromagnetic energies. Perhaps, then, the color that pleases us most resonates on our own wavelength—the one that we are most in tune with.

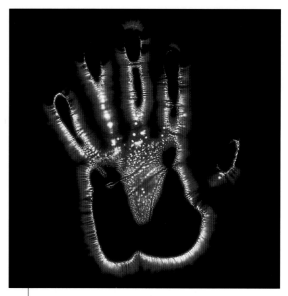

Kirlian photography is a technique that captures the auric energy given out by the body. Here, a human hand is revealed to be glowing with life and vitality.

Fields of color

It is possible, too, that the color we respond to best is the one that is most predominant in our auras—the many-colored field of radiation that encircles our bodies. The aura is made up of a ring of colors that correspond to our feelings and emotions. The most noticeable color in a person's aura reveals his or her prevailing mood and disposition. We may not be able to see our own auras, but we do identify with their colors, and it could be this match that we intuitively pick out as our favorite color. (You can find out more about the aura on pages 66–71.)

Matching characteristics

Color therapists have discovered a link between color and personality. They have shown that extroverted people—those who are active, out-going and exuberant—tend to be drawn to bright, vibrant colors, whereas the more introverted among us—those who are inclined to be shy, sensitive, and cautious—on the whole favor the quieter, more restful colors.

Each color, it seems, has its own definite set of characteristics. When we are attracted to a color, we are attracted to its "character." Moreover, we are attracted to it because we identify with its characteristics and recognize those qualities in ourselves. You could say that your favorite color is a mirror of you.

Children often prefer the colors at the brighter end of the spectrum, yellow being the most popular choice. Adults tend to opt for blues more often. Perhaps such changes reflect our mental development, acquisition of new skills and interests, or changing chemical processes that take place naturally as we age.

So, next time you tell someone what your favorite color is, beware—you may be disclosing a good deal more about your innermost self than you might think!

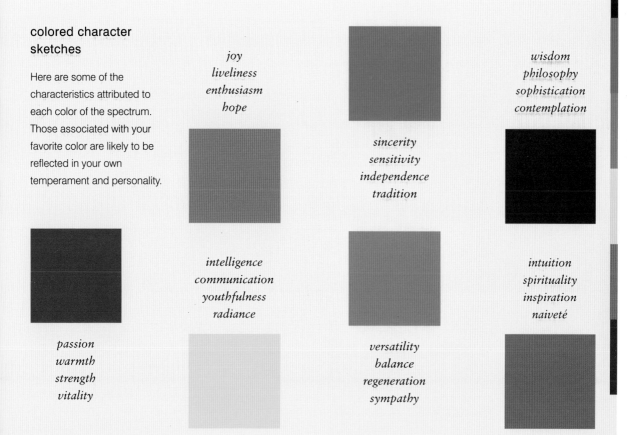

colored character sketches

Here are some of the characteristics attributed to each color of the spectrum. Those associated with your favorite color are likely to be reflected in your own temperament and personality.

joy
liveliness
enthusiasm
hope

wisdom
philosophy
sophistication
contemplation

sincerity
sensitivity
independence
tradition

intelligence
communication
youthfulness
radiance

intuition
spirituality
inspiration
naiveté

passion
warmth
strength
vitality

versatility
balance
regeneration
sympathy

Red

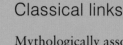

The color of passion and vitality

Vital and dramatic, red is the symbol of fire and masculinity, of energy and power. As a color, it evokes intense passions including love, hatred, anger, and blind rage.

Here, at the hot end of the spectrum, is the most positive of vibrations, a dynamic expression belonging to powerful leaders, to men and women of strength and determination. Purposeful and self-assertive, red insists on initiating action. Without hesitation, it takes charge and directs.

Classical links

Mythologically associated with Mars, the god of war, this color conveys raw aggression, its savagery described in Nature's "red in tooth and claw." For red can rend and destroy and as such has become the symbol of revolution—a metaphor for the spilling of blood in the name of a collective cause. In the modern idiom, red has become inalienably linked with radical ideals and is associated politically with socialist movements throughout the world.

But red is also symbolic of Apollo, the Sun god, who drives his blazing chariot across the midday skies, evoking the shimmering heat at the height of a summer's afternoon. And even in the cold of winter, red has the power to warm and to energize. Snuggle under a crimson blanket, pull on a scarlet sweater, slip your hands into a pair of cherry-colored mittens, and you will instantly feel the warming rays penetrating through the chill to your bones.

The sign of danger

Because of its long wavelength, there is an immediacy in red that cannot be ignored. Walk into a room in a red gown, and all heads will

Sporty and active, red is the color that stimulates, that warms and cheers, that gives us energy and peps us up. Red says to yourself and to the world: "Get out there and take control."

The color of sex and passion

Representing the physical and material realms, the color red is symbolic of the procreative urge, stimulating passionate responses and feelings of lust. Red and sexual activity are inextricably linked. Think of "red-light" districts, or of nightclubs so often favor this color as part of their décor. For red brings out our most extroverted impulses and encourages us to abandon our inhibitions and throw caution to the wind.

Variations on a theme

Pink, a softer, more subtle expression of this color, has a reputation for promoting gentle, loving feelings. When red is too harsh, pink is no less uplifting, but it works in a more understated fashion. Here is a useful color to help tone up the circulation, to make the body feel warm, and to pep up the spirits when one is down or depressed. Moreover, pink is the color of rejuvenation and encourages youthful vigor well into old age.

automatically turn. For red calls attention to itself. It arouses the senses, quickens the pulse, and excites the emotions. As the "get up and go" color, it energizes, motivates, and galvanizes us into action, and it is this factor that has awarded red its universal acknowledgment as the symbol of danger. Indeed, signs of warning, traffic lights that compel us to stop, or signals that alert us to hazards ahead are invariably printed in red. Emergency equipment and fire-fighting vehicles, too, come more often than not in a vivid red. For the vibrancy of red compels. It demands we take heed. Ignore it at your peril.

images of red

- *the sun setting in the evening sky*
- *poppy petals blowing in the breeze*
- *the flame of a blazing log fire*
- *a fire engine racing to the rescue*

expressions of red

- *red rag to a bull*
- *painting the town red*
- *red-letter day*
- *seeing red*
- *a red-blooded male (or female!)*

Orange

The color of joy and hope

Combining the physical passion of red with the mental detachment of yellow, orange induces spontaneous action, enthusiasm, and quick wits. Like a soda pop, orange positively fizzes with life. It is the ray that brings joy to the heart. Happy and exultant, orange introduces a note of celebration and carries us away to dizzy heights on a burst of euphoria.

Boosting morale

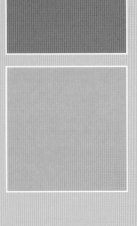

Being adjacent to red on the spectrum, orange possesses powers of energy and enthusiasm similar to those emitted by its neighbor, but with less of that brash forcefulness. Here is a powerful morale-booster, a color that will replace the missing vital spark. Use orange to enliven and revitalize your jaded spirits. When you are tired or off-color, yet still expected to go the extra mile, orange will provide the life-force necessary for you to carry on. Or else, at the end of a tiring day, envelop yourself in a coral-colored wrap and feel the sparkle of hope and optimism return as your cares and stresses slowly ebb away.

The color of free expression

Radiating exuberance, this color vibration symbolizes happiness and engenders feelings of conviviality. For orange is an agreeable color—tolerant, good-natured, and easy to please. In encouraging sociability, orange releases our channels of communication and brings forth freedom of expression. Absorbing as it does some of the influence of yellow, the next color in line, orange aids concentration and stimulates the development of ideas. When information needs to be committed to memory, think orange. And think orange again when difficult decisions have to be made, when initiative is required to take advantage of opportunities, or when sustained efforts are called for in order to bring crucial projects to fruition.

Social, fun-loving, and vitalizing, orange gets us moving and positively fizzes with exuberance and life. Let orange into your life and release your creativity and communication skills.

Hot spice

The restorative pep and health-giving properties of orange are nowhere more in evidence than in the spice rack! Check out paprika, with its heart-warming, rich color and aromatic peppery flavor. Cayenne for its stimulating heat, which warms a chill in wintertime, aids digestion and boosts a sluggish circulation. Ginger, with its zing and zest, putting an exotic kick into any dish. Or saffron-colored, subtle, and distinctly-flavored turmeric, long associated with sun worship and indispensable both in the kitchen, for curries and rice, and in the medicine cabinet for treating cuts and wounds.

Youthful fun

In orange we see a youthful *joie de vivre*, a love of movement and dance, and a spontaneous desire for enjoyment and fun. Orange has the power to blend the spiritual with the sexual. It is an inspirational color which broadens the mind, brings people together, and makes social occasions go with a swing.

The Midas touch

Central to the essence of orange lies a core of generosity. For this color gives out in a big way, broadcasting to all and sundry its bighearted magnanimity. Orange fosters good feelings, and as it does so, it attracts back to itself positive beneficence. It is no coincidence that, in the art of Feng Shui, the Chinese recognize the magnetic qualities of this color, and advocate the keeping of goldfish to enhance the wealth of the household. For indeed, orange has traditionally enjoyed a long association with prosperity and well-being.

images of orange

- *marmalade spread on hot, buttered toast*
- *goldfish shimmering in a glassy pool*
- *tangerines hanging like miniature lanterns on a citrus tree*
- *the robes of a Buddhist monk*
- *a jack-o'-lantern*
- *fresh juice and toast*
- *gingerbread men*

expression of orange

- *the spice of life*

Yellow

The color of intelligence and communication

Because yellow reflects so much light back to the eye, it possesses, perhaps more than any other color, a radiance that reaches out like a beacon in the dead of night. Yellow proclaims itself from afar. It is an unmissable color which shouts its happiness for all to see and hear. With its busy qualities and child-like instincts, yellow refuses to keep still. It is a veritable "pick-me-up"— a color that animates, enlivens, energizes, and puts a positive bounce in our step. Lighthearted and carefree, yellow is the ray of sunshine that, on dull mornings in late winter, suddenly breaks through the clouds and promises us the cheer to come.

The master juggler

For yellow, variety is the spice of life. Characterized by a low boredom threshold and manifested by impatience, this expression requires novelty and change. Fleet of foot and nimble of mind, yellow seeks a multiplicity of interests and a wide social network for stimulation. Under its aegis, the tendency to flit from topic to topic, from one interest to the next, and from one relationship to another may result in a superficiality that skims the surface of experience, leaving an understanding that is only skin-deep. But yellow is a master juggler, adept at the balancing act and able to sustain five conversations at the same time without, even for a moment, losing the thread of any. With its practiced dexterity, yellow has the ability to keep several pots on the boil at any given time.

Carrying the message

The most significant association of yellow is with the mind, for this color has long enjoyed an affinity with knowledge and all cerebral processes. As such, yellow represents intelligence, stimulates mental activity, and encourages rational thinking. In ancient mythology, yellow was the color assigned to Mercury, the messenger of the gods, and thus has acquired rulership over all forms of communication. Creative, imaginative, and original in thought and ideas, yellow is essentially clever and quick-witted, an inspirational color for those of an inquiring mind. Think yellow when faced with a decision, when a judgment calls to be weighed in the balance, or even when a simple winning slogan is required.

Fast and mercurial, yellow stimulates the mind and is associated with intelligence. Paint your office yellow to influence discussion and encourage the rapid flow of new ideas.

Word power

Yellow is fundamentally non violent, and perhaps it is precisely because of its association with the intellect, rather than with physical prowess, that it has come to represent cowardice. For, in conflict situations, yellow would not prefer to resort to fisticuffs, but would rather use words to sort out its differences. As far as yellow is concerned, the pen is assuredly mightier than the sword.

Optimistic and sociable

Colors are often associated with different parts of the body, and yellow is no exception. The nervous system comes under the aegis of this color and different types of yellow exert different influences. Too green or acid a yellow can jar the nerves, whereas the deeper the shade, the more it helps to settle the emotions. Yellow is young and fun-loving. A sociable color which encourages friendship, yellow brings warm and energizing sunshine into our lives, awakens the senses, and radiates optimism and good cheer.

Intellect versus emotion

As the color of the intellect, yellow encourages detachment from our emotions. It gives us the strength to distance ourselves from our feelings and to rationalize what is going on around us in our lives. Yellow is a color that is, therefore, invaluable in times of personal difficulty, as it prompts us to stand back from our problems in order to view our situation from a new and more logical perspective. Moreover, yellow gives us the courage to let go.

images of yellow

- *a lighthouse beacon flashing its signal across the raging seas*
- *pollen grains dusted on the wings of a bee*
- *a shaft of golden sunlight breaking through the trees*
- *a dazzling field of sunflowers*

expressions of yellow

- *golden mean*
- *yellow-bellied*
- *mellow yellow*

Green

The color of Nature, of verdant foliage and lush vegetation, and the symbol of fertility, green facilitates life and growth. From the early green shoots appearing in the spring, the greening of the land heralds the cyclical nature of time—the birth, death, and subsequent re-growth as season follows upon season. Thus it is that green has come to represent the concept of regeneration and renewal, a perpetual wheel of motion driven by a strict order that underlies the laws of the universe and that produces the evergreen of life.

A question of balance

Just as in Nature, green is the universal balancer, harmonizing with all colors. So, falling in the spectrum between yellow and blue, green brings together the joy of the former and the serenity of the latter. Taking also from its neighbors the childlike wonder of the first and the sobriety of the other, green builds a bridge between the folly of youth and the maturity of experience. In the final analysis, green combines hope with intellect and enthusiasm with pragmatism. It blends them in a metaphysical mix to produce, in its own essence, the wisdom of discernment and a judgment that is balanced and true.

Inexperience of youth

And yet, despite its spiritually enriching qualities, there is another side to green which it has perhaps absorbed from yellow, its youthful neighbor, and which has given rise to green's reputation for naiveté. For, to be called "green" implies the ingenuousness and immaturity we that associate with the innocence of a child.

A green thought in a green shade

Green is the fulcrum, the midpoint where the warm colors of red, orange, and yellow end and the cool colors of blue, indigo, and violet begin. Here, between the two, is an oasis of peace and tranquility, where spirits are soothed and emotions becalmed. Enfolded by green, we are

Quintessentially the color of Nature, green has the power to calm and quietly inspire the creative processes to take form and shape. As the fulcrum color, green also brings balance and harmony.

room's green interior, taking its influence from the soothing effects of a cool glade, is designed precisely as a haven to calm the nerves and gently foster dramatic or musical imagination.

Symbol of peace

Green can also symbolize peace, in the shape of an olive branch, offered in the hope of building a new understanding by which men and women can live together in perfect harmony and accord.

The color of enchantment

Because of its association with fairies, green is considered by some people to be an unlucky color. Many refuse to drive a green car or to paint their front door any shade of green. According to tradition, sending a get-well card that contains the color green is regarded as highly inauspicious and bodes ill indeed. For this color, to the superstitious, augurs worsening health and beckons the recipient toward a hasty departure to the other world.

afforded time, space, and a place of restfulness where our souls are free to soar to creative heights and our imaginations, like sown seeds, can burst forth into life.

Theater of the soul

Traditionally decorated in green, the "green room" in theaters, concert halls, and television studios, is a room that is situated close to the stage, specifically for the actors' or musicians' use. Here, performers go to collect their thoughts, or perhaps to gather inspiration, either before or between performances. The

images of green

○ *the green iridescence on a kingfisher's wing*
○ *a leafy glade on a summer's morn*
○ *emeralds glistening in an empress' crown*
○ *a golf course on a sunny day*

expressions of green

○ *to give the green light*
○ *green thumb*
○ *the green-eyed monster*
○ *wearing of the green*
○ *a green old age*

Blue

The color of
sensitivity and
loyalty

With blue comes calmness and personal dignity. Here, at the "cool" end of the spectrum, we find our minds bent on higher thoughts as blue connects us with the mystical side of our beings. Philosophy and intuition come under the aegis of this color, raising our consciousness to esoteric heights. Blue symbolizes sensitivity. It asks us to look inside ourselves, promotes our sincerity, encourages our devotions, and assists us in our meditations.

The essence of duty

Blue takes a tempered approach. Not for this color the impetuous pushiness of red, or the high spirits of orange, or even the youthful playfulness of yellow. In blue there is an innate conservatism, a desire for safety, for peace and security. With blue we acquire the ability to become objective, to take a dispassionate view of life. Blue teaches us to learn, to

watch from the wings, to lay our plans, to buckle down and reach our goals. For blue is innately ambitious and symbolizes both duty and responsibility. Consider for a moment the steely resolve and focused determination of blue-gray. Or the uplifting aspirations of celestial azure which instantly flies us up to the heavens. Or the steadying influence and organizational ability of navy. In all its variations, blue instills loyalty, sincerity, and trustworthiness. It demands truth and perfection, and offers both kindness and understanding in return.

Integrity and truth

It is perhaps because blue, especially navy blue, projects a central core of confidence and efficiency that it is so often used as the color for uniforms. Whether in the armed forces, the financial sector, or the business world, dark blue

Fluid and celestial, blue cools and refreshes as it brings to mind the wide expanses of sea and sky. Although calming in moderation, too much blue may make us overtired, or even depressed.

bedroom décor. But too much blue here presents a problem—namely shaking off sluggishness come morning, when we must rise and shine. Remember, blue is not an energizer, and it requires a strong dash of color from the warmer end of the spectrum to bring the senses alive. For too great an expanse of blue tires the spirit and depresses the soul.

Singing the blues

Blue is deeply introspective. It turns our thoughts inwards and inclines us to brood. We say that loneliness and melancholia put us in a "blue mood." Indeed, this is the sadness that has given birth to a whole genre of music so powerful that it scours the soul. Through "the Blues," so aptly descriptive of the torment that our feelings can bring us, we experience the suffering of generations and hear coming down through the ages the desolate echoes of misery and sorrow that are interwoven into the rich emotional fabric that makes up the human condition.

is seen to carry authority and integrity. But another reason for blue's virtuous reputation may lie in its esoteric significance as a color that contains antiseptic and astringent properties, with the power to counteract contamination. May it be, then, that metaphorically we see in blue a moral incorruptibility, conveying to us ethical high-mindedness and truth?

Deep sleep

The calming vibrations of blue relax the muscles, quieten the mind, and send us to sleep. No wonder, then, that this is a popular color in

images of blue

- *the brilliant blue of a bay on an azure coast*
- *a bluebell wood in early May*
- *squares of lapis lazuli set into a priceless Byzantine mosaic*
- *a cloudless summer's-day sky*

expressions of blue

- *bluebird of happiness*
- *once in a blue moon*
- *out of the blue*
- *feeling blue*

Indigo

The color of contemplation and intuition

Associated with dreams and the unconscious mind, the intense depths of indigo lead us through the deep-set labyrinths of awareness to the very margins of human understanding. As the color of the vast midnight skies, indigo presents us with infinity, the never-ending expanses of the universe, and asks us to question our existence in the eternal scheme of things. Looking into indigo takes us on a journey into the unknown.

New age

As we step into a new millennium, indigo wraps us in its folds and offers reassurance as it opens a gateway to the future. How strange to consider that, in preparation for this new age, we have seen in the latter part of the twentieth century how denim, dyed with indigo, has become the ubiquitous dress of the young. So it is that indigo has come to symbolize youth, the growth of awareness, and the promise of tomorrow's flower. Indeed, as the very concepts of flower power, of making love not war, of transcendental meditation and consciousness-raising have become synonymous with the decades leading up to the New Age, so these same themes may be said equally to embody all that is quintessentially indigo.

Awakening

With indigo we feel we can tap into seemingly boundless reserves of knowledge and dip our toes into the collective unconscious. This color is associated with heightened psychic powers and advanced spiritual perception. Meditating with indigo in mind will awaken our intuitive processes and sharpen our abilities to make clear and well-informed decisions. The reflective qualities of this color prompt us to expand our minds and to take in the wider issues of our society. When preparing for

Indigo brings us infinity and depth. A contemplative color, it takes us deep into our subconscious mind, making us ponder the wonders of our world and break free of psychological fetters.

a business deal, when undertaking research, or even when simply beginning a new project, contemplating indigo will enable us to see the broader picture and will put our work into proper perspective.

Moving on

Indigo encourages us to shed what we no longer require, to rid ourselves of the physical and emotional baggage that is holding back our progress along our chosen paths. Indigo asks us to face our fears and phobias, to look squarely into the threatening shadows that cast their gloom over our lives. Whether it is that we are held back by our own inhibitions, or trapped by the circumstances, situation, or people that we find ourselves among, indigo symbolizes the strength that we need to conquer our weaknesses, to break free and move on.

Deep blue

Moving farther along the continuum of the "cool" colors, in indigo's deep blue we can sense profound and limitless calm. Here is the wisdom of the ages, mature understanding and balanced reasoning. Here are the patience of Job and the judgment of Solomon rolled into one. Here are empathy and fellow-feeling, a place of safety into which we can pour our troubles and know that we will be heard. But a word of caution is required. Though indigo's virtues are many, dwelling too long in its soporific environment can induce self-absorption and over-sentimentality. Golden yellow makes an ideal companion to this color, adding pep and stimulus to unfold our creativity and imagination.

images of indigo

- *the midnight sky studded with a million stars*
- *ink from the squid as it baffles its prey*
- *a pile of jeans folded on a market stall*

expressions of indigo

- *burn the midnight oil*
- *"Mood Indigo" (a classic song)*

Violet

At the farthest end from materialistic red, violet presents us with the highest expression of spirituality. Here are united intelligence and understanding, for this is a farsighted color, pregnant with both sensitivity and spirituality and suffused with psychic power. Violet endows us with generosity of spirit and teaches us the blessings of our unselfish actions. With violet we learn to trust our instincts, to become independent and free, to break with tradition, and to allow our minds to soar with confidence into territories untested and untried.

The color of kings

Historically, violet and purple have been held in great esteem as high–status colors and are traditionally considered to be the emblem of royalty, of spiritual leadership, and of officials of state. The Ancient Romans extracted this pigment from shellfish, and thus it was the most expensive dye and the color best symbolizing pomp and circumstance. Violet and purple, in particular, have long been associated with ceremony and have been much used through the centuries in ritual and religious services.

But, as in all things, moderation is called for when dealing with this color, because a surfeit of violet can turn its grandeur into pomposity and its dignity into arrogance. Be aware that, in its negative expression, violet can ferment an over-inflated estimation of one's abilities and station in life.

Raising its profile

Although out of favor as an interior design color for much of the twentieth century, except in some of the gloomy schemes typical of the 'seventies, violet is now beginning to sweep its way into our homes and taking its rightful place in the world of decoration and design. Interestingly, this strong color is affiliated with Uranus, which represents supreme idealism and humanitarian zeal. So perhaps it is no coincidence that violet should be making its entrance now just as Uranus, also known as the Great Awakener, is ushering in the Age of Aquarius.

Rich, regal, and voluptuously sensual, violet is also the color of the higher mind and evokes intuition and spirituality. Violet lets us stretch our wings and fly toward a new horizon.

Flights of fancy

Beloved by artists, who recognize this color's power to heighten creative expression, violet transports us to a fantasy world filled with wonder and delight. In its rich sensuality, violet conjures the opulence of silk, the sumptuousness of velvet, and the liquid rhapsody that is the taste of melting chocolate.

The eternal paradox

That violet is derived from a mixture of blue and red, colors found on opposing sides of the color wheel, implies that at the core of this color lie potentially irreconcilable differences. In violet come together passion and intellect, dreams and reality. Illusion is coupled with practicality, and vision with experience which is very much anchored in the here and now.

Shades of difference

The lighter, more delicate, shades of violet such as lilac and lavender have the power to release our memories and gently take us back to a former time of grace and gentility. For these colors are essentially charming, their very names redolent of old-fashioned fragrances that fill our senses and return us to our childhood days. The resplendence of magenta evokes the emotions of adolescence, with their lofty ideals and their steps into early independence. Magenta allows us to experiment with who we are and gives us the courage to be flexible and to discover our own identity. Then, with mauve, we are taken to full-blown maturity, as the added blue contributes to our worldly experience and our recognition of all that is divine.

images of violet

○ *pendulous racemes of wisteria flowers, frothy and fragrant on the vine*
○ *jagged streaks of purple lightning in an electric storm*
○ *vivid streaks of violet across the sky when the sun finally sinks after the day is done*

expressions of violet

○ *born to the purple*
○ *shrinking violet*
○ *purple with rage*

White

> ### The color of light and purity

With white we experience the total sum of all things. For here is the softness of a newborn lamb, the lightness of a feather, and the incandescent beauty of a pearl. But here, too, is the cold of ice, the crispness of frost and the hardness of marble. From gossamer clouds to jagged snow-capped mountains, and from the sweetness of sugar to the brackish taste of salt, we see in white many sharp contrasts.

Snow white

White conjures the stillness and silence when dawn breaks over the snow-covered land after a blizzard in the night. And, just like that untrodden blanket of snow, white brings to mind quintessential purity. Untainted and unsullied, angelic white reflects perfection, virginal innocence, and the incorruptibility of true goodness.

Good versus evil

Since light is essentially white, this color symbolizes "enlightenment" and carries the wisdom of the ages. Indeed, white represents all that is positive and has the power to turn evil into good. A white flag, for example, announces a truce in hostilities. White magic works in harmony with Nature, harnessing its forces in order to bring about benefits for mankind. A white lie is a falsehood that has the purpose of protecting someone's feelings.

Prim and proper

As a color in itself, white is clean and crisp and fresh and, as such, conveys a strong sense of cleanliness and hygiene. But there is also a starkness in white that brings out a clinical detachment and that keeps emotion at arm's length. White may be sophisticated, but, like stiff collars and cuffs, it can also be formal and starchy.

Freshness is synonymous with white, its essence captured in snowdrops breaking through the frozen ground.

images of white

- *confectioners' sugar dusted over a chocolate cake*
- *the first snowdrop breaking through the frozen soil*
- *white linen sheets billowing on the line*

expressions of white

- *white as a sheet*
- *white elephant*
- *the Great White Way*

Black

The color of seduction and sophistication

Because black absorbs all colors and reflects nothing back, it has traditionally been associated with everything that is considered negative and corrupt. With black there is an absence of light: an oppressive, all-enveloping and all-pervading darkness that restricts and confines. For black obscures goodness and truth. Along with this comes its reputation for representing sexy sophistication and daring, exciting deeds.

Witchcraft

Black has long been synonomous with matters that are sinister and downright wicked. As opposed to the glowing choir of celestial angels, Satan is traditionally depicted as a dark figure. Involvement in diabolic deeds is referred to as the practice of the black arts. And black magic, a form of the occult that itself describes something "that is hidden," perverts the laws of Nature by its association with witchcraft and evil spirits.

A black humor

Black portrays doom and gloom, the "black dog" of depression that takes us to the very depths of despondency. It is the poisonous black mamba snake and the black widow spider, whose venom can kill. When things look black, we know we face a difficult situation and the going will be tough. Black is no laughing matter, and even in comedy, it describes the absurd and the macabre, juxtaposing, as it does, the ghoulish with the amusing.

The color of fashion

But another side of black brings out its element of the seductive and enigmatic that ranks it as one of the most sophisticated of colors. From lacy lingerie to leather jackets, black is decidedly sexy. Black is the cocktail dress or tailcoat of the socialite. And black is the color of chic which one is certain will never be out of fashion.

Black has long been considered the most seductive of colors—a fashion color that never loses its sex appeal.

images of black

- *shadows in the midday sun*
- *the panther stealthily stalking its prey*
- *a polished table fashioned from the wood of the ebony tree*

expressions of black

- *the Black Death*
- *black as coal*
- *the black sheep of the family*

Colors that sell

A product has
only a quarter
of a second to
catch our eye

Think of yourself pushing a cart around a supermarket. Your eyes are constantly darting from one object to another, taking in a steady stream of information and settling on the brands you know just long enough to give you time to reach out a hand and pick them off the shelf.

It has been estimated that, in order to attract our attention as shoppers, a product has only a quarter of a second to catch our eye before our gaze moves on. That split second is crucial in selling a product.

The first line of attack in catching our eye must lie in the packaging, for this not only serves as the magnet that draws the attention but also conveys the essential information that the would-be purchaser requires to make a decision as to whether to buy the product or not.

Packaging and color

Color is the most powerful component of any package. Indeed, when a new product is launched, a great deal of money and research go into its image and presentation and, most importantly, into the choice of color combination employed in the design and lettering of the packaging.

Color plays a number of important roles in the marketing of a product. Research has shown that it is color that first attracts the shopper's attention to a particular brand. Color also maintains the shopper's interest and is identified with that product ever after in the shopper's mind. Because we attach specific qualities to certain colors (see table opposite), consumers instantly pick up messages put out by the manufacturer.

The message in the color

Because we so strongly associate certain colors with specific concepts or images, the colors themselves have come to embody those ideas—so much so that a color is often sufficient in itself to communicate the message of the image it represents. Youth may be symbolized by bright orange, sunshine yellow, or acid green. Elegance is encapsulated in pale grays, jade and aqua tints. A sense of tradition may be portrayed by brown, ochre, and mustard yellow, as opposed to futuristic space-age, which is better described by silver, violet, and electric blue. Femininity may be seen in pastels and masculinity in strong, dark colors.

Getting the idea across

Advertising and product designers recognize the power of color association and put it to use in their work. They know that in the packaging of merchandise it is essential to match a product with the appropriate color in order to get the right image across and to attract the right consumer group. Getting the color wrong may sound the death knell for the product itself.

International appeal

When designs are for an international market, designers need to remember that not all color associations are universal, and some do not necessarily travel across borders with ease.

What may signify happiness in one country may be linked with sorrow in another. To the French, red symbolizes masculinity, whereas in certain parts of Africa, it represents death. And in other parts of the world, such as the countries of South America, it is not red but purple that is associated with funerals and the ending of life. In the West, green is usually linked with conservation and environmental issues. But in Muslim countries this color is sacrosanct and should not be exploited in commerce. Travelers will almost certainly notice that local packaging looks unfamiliar, because the power of color crosses boundaries but its associations do not.

cool color range

suitable for:

- cosmetics
- skin-care products
- toiletries
- cleaning products
- dairy products
- frozen foods
- pharmaceuticals
- bottled mineral water

associated with:

- coolness
- freshness
- hygiene
- purity
- good health
- quenching thirst
- tangy flavors
- sophistication
- lightness
- reassurance

blue ○ green ○ white ○ pale gray ○ aqua

warm color range

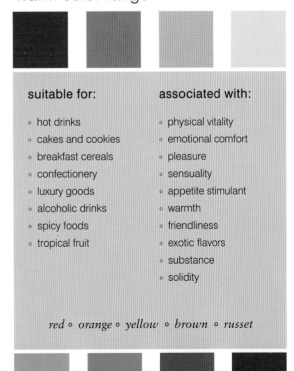

suitable for:

- hot drinks
- cakes and cookies
- breakfast cereals
- confectionery
- luxury goods
- alcoholic drinks
- spicy foods
- tropical fruit

associated with:

- physical vitality
- emotional comfort
- pleasure
- sensuality
- appetite stimulant
- warmth
- friendliness
- exotic flavors
- substance
- solidity

red ○ orange ○ yellow ○ brown ○ russet

Color in interior design

Color in our home is integral to our well-being

There is little that has the power to transform both our mood and the atmosphere of our environment as quickly as color can. With color, whether in the form of paint, fabrics, or accessories, we can change our moods in a flash—lift our spirits when we are in the doldrums, feel warm in the gloomy depths of winter, or soothe our frayed tempers after a trying day. With color, too, we can virtually change the shape and size of a room, making salient features stand out or camouflaging unsightly ones from view. All you need to perform this magic is a little insider knowledge on how to make color work in your home.

Bringing colors together

When decorating a room, consider the three levels that have to interact in order to produce a successful color scheme:

○ **Background colors** *are the main, base colors—those that are used on walls, floors and ceilings.*

○ **Foreground colors** *are introduced through fabrics and upholstery, via draperies and rugs, or by linen for the table or the bed.*

○ **Accent colors** *are the highlights of color that are found in ornaments, pictures or lampshades, which either harmonize with the background or provide a pleasing contrast.*

Whether you begin with the background, foreground, or accent colors, pull together the other two levels in order to achieve a complete look. Work with the same tonal density and range of colors, introducing shades that blend or contrast, all the time keeping in mind the style, look, atmosphere, and effect you want to create.

Color tricks

Color in the home plays a central role in establishing the quality of light in our living environment. With a few tricks it is possible not only to transform the ambience of a room, but also to alter its dimensions visually:

○ High ceilings can be "lowered" with a dark color.
○ Ceilings and floors in the same light-colored hue will make a room look bigger.
○ Narrow rooms can be "widened" by painting the short-end walls a dark color and the two adjoining walls in a lighter shade.
○ Cold rooms can be "warmed up" with peach, coral, pink, red or sunshine-yellow paint or accessories.
○ Hot rooms that get direct sunlight can be "cooled" with light blues, greens, and whites.
○ Big rooms can be made to feel cozier by painting the walls and ceilings with dark, warm colors.
○ Painting small rooms in a pale shade makes them appear larger.
○ Cream, pale lilac, or light blue on the far wall will "lengthen" a short hallway.

monochromatic color scheme

harmonious color scheme

Using different tones and shades of the same color in a room can create a very stylish effect. Consider navy supported by turquoise blue, violet teamed with lilac, or olive green with lime. Monochromatic color schemes like these can produce very positive results, especially when different textures are introduced. But to add real interest and definition here, a strong focal color needs to be picked out as an accent in cushions, vases, or rugs, otherwise the look may be in danger of appearing monotonous and dull.

Two colors that are situated next to each other on the color wheel (see pages 10–11) are "related" and work well together in interior design schemes because they are in harmony with each other. Think, for example, how pleasing to the eye violet and magenta are when they are used together, or yellow with green. It is essential to match the tones here to create a relaxing atmosphere, but the occasional accent of contrasting color will add the essential zing that brings these partnerships alive.

contrasting color scheme

Using two colors that lie directly opposite each other on the color wheel can produce a vibrant and exciting effect. However, this type of scheme can be tricky to use well unless the contrasting colors are chosen correctly. Choosing pure colors, for instance, can be very jarring visually, whereas two opposing *tints* will give a strong effect without unduly upsetting the eye. Think of the dazzle of primary red and green, but take another look at the complementary partnership of smoky pink and jade. Bringing in a color that harmonizes with one of the chosen pair will marry the look together and ease any clashing that might otherwise have occurred. Plan carefully before you leap. Start out with a basic color idea, and then see what subtle variations you can devise.

using neutrals

Neutrals—such as white, cream and, beige—are useful as a background canvas and can be built on by adding a range of accent colors to produce dramatically different styles and atmospheres. The addition of pale gray or ice blue will give a sophisticated look. Alternatively, a bolder theme can be achieved by overlaying hot, spicy splashes of color. With cool tones, neutral colors create a calm and soothing atmosphere and give the smallest room a sense of space. Teamed with more exotic colors, neutrals will take the intensity out of the atmosphere and provide a welcome balance. If used in dark or north-facing rooms, however, neutrals can be lifeless and may need to be pepped up with brighter colors.

Living with color: Red

Energizing, warm, and opulent, red pumps up the heart rate and generates an atmosphere of excitement. Stronger shades of red can prove overpowering in the home, so are best used where you want to promote energy, but not where a calm and soothing ambience is required. As it is an "advancing" color, red tends to make large rooms look smaller.

hallway

Reds are excellent shades to use in hallways and corridors, generating a warm, welcoming feeling in lobbies and entrances. As this is a "fast" color, it will encourage speedy through-movement and so discourage crowds gathering in doorways or areas of access.

bedroom

Sexy and passionate, red arouses the emotions and encourages love-making. At other times, though, it can lead to restlessness and insomnia. All things considered, it is perhaps not the best color to choose for this particular room.

dining room

In terms of stimulating appetite and conversation, red is a good triggering color. So, in the dining room, it will induce lively discussion and appreciative diners. However, use red sparingly even in this room, as too much can lead to irritation, rushed meals, and indigestion.

living room

After long exposure, the excitement of red begins to irritate, so it is not a good color for a sitting room where the family will want to spend a lot of time relaxing together. Vivid reds can lead to headaches and bad tempers. If you want a warm color here, choose pink or coral instead.

kitchen

Since kitchens can be hot places, too much red here can rev up the temperature to intolerable levels. Spots of red used as an accent color will help to warm up a room with little sunlight, but since a little red goes a long way, it is best used sparingly.

bathroom

Red might be fine for taking a brisk shower, but it is not really conducive to a long, luxurious, relaxing soak in the tub.

Blue

With its power to soothe and quieten, blue is arguably the most relaxing of colors. But it is also remarkably versatile, from its palest shades, which create elegance and space, to the deeper hues which evoke the drama of midnight skies. Cool, expansive, bright, fresh or formal, there is a shade of blue to fit almost any situation.

hallway

Some shades of blue can prove too cool and somber for corridors and should ideally be teamed with warmer shades to give a more welcoming glow. House fronts and doorways painted in French navy and white never fail to give a smart and businesslike appearance to any residence.

bedroom

With its quietening influence and restful effect, blue is an ideal color choice for a bedroom. Remember, however, that if you tend to while away long periods of time in your bedroom, too much blue might bring on a melancholic turn of mind.

dining room

It is generally held that blue does not lend itself to the dining room. Perhaps one reason is that there are very few foods that are truly blue. Research has shown that blue does not readily stimulate the appetite. So, if used here, it needs to be applied as a warmer tone, mixed with red or pink.

living room

While it is true that blue is a restful color, a concentration of it here can have a deeply sobering effect and bring out the more introspective side of the personality. Lighter shades of blue work better in the living area, particularly if the room gets direct sunlight.

kitchen

Blue teamed with white is a popular choice for the kitchen. But too much blue in this environment has a tendency to slow down time, making the whole process of cooking seem to take longer than necessary. Turquoise is more invigorating and uplifting here, especially when teamed with orange.

bathroom

Blue's association with water makes it a natural choice for bathrooms and powder rooms. However, the shade needs to be selected wisely. Blue has a soporific effect, so the deeper shades may not be suitable. Aquamarine and turquoise are more enlivening alternatives and are reminders of the freshness of the sea.

Living with color: Yellow

Cheerful and cheering, yellow lifts the spirits and promotes warmth and well-being. But it can also prove cool and acidic, so choosing the right shade for the effect required needs careful attention. In general, though, yellow stimulates creative ideas, so it is a valuable color in studies, offices, or other places of learning.

hallway

Golds and yellows—with their abilities to animate and cheer—are excellent, highly welcoming choices for entrance halls, waiting rooms, and any areas where people tend to congregate.

bedroom

With its bracing effects, too much yellow in the bedroom is not conducive to a good night's sleep. To avoid jangling the nerves, use it here as an accent color, lifting blue, for example, with touches of gold.

dining room

Here, crocus yellow will exude a pleasant, friendly feeling, engendering a sense of bonhomie and well-being at mealtimes. Moreover, it will give out a warm glow whatever the time of year—especially useful if the natural light in this room is poor.

living room

From palest primrose, through sumptuous gold, to rich earthy ochre, yellow fills a room with Mediterranean light. Choose bright shades to bring a smile to a sitting room with poor light; but do not forget that yellow is also an invigorating color, so choose deeper, earthier tones to sit back and mellow out.

kitchen

Bright and refreshing, creamy yellow brings the sunshine into a kitchen without the danger of overheating the atmosphere. A warm, vibrant shade works well here and can be relied upon to provide that wide-awake feeling at any time of day.

bathroom

Fresh and zingy, citrus yellow will wake you up and put a spring in your step first thing in the morning. However, this might not be the color for you if your bathroom is the main place you go to relax away the stresses of the day.

Green

Just as in Nature, where green is the backdrop to all other colors, so in our homes it can provide the background for any color scheme. Green is also flexible and adaptable, able to create a multitude of effects from vivid and bracing to soft and relaxing. Whether the atmosphere required is elegant or zany, restful or invigorating, green will lend itself to the job.

hallway

As the color that is the easiest for the eye, green offers a soothing and non-confrontational welcome into any home. Greet visitors with an aura of harmony and peace!

bedroom

With its restorative powers, light green is an excellent choice for the bedroom and brings peace and relaxation to its inhabitants. Beware of this hue, however, as too strong or deep a green can be somewhat sluggish and requires warmer accents to help enliven the atmosphere.

dining room

When there is plenty of natural light streaming into this room, a warm green here can make even the smallest dining room appear airy and spacious. Try jade and cream for that homely apple-pie atmosphere, or sharpen the taste buds with lime splashed with yellow and red.

living room

Where the light is plentiful and the ceilings high, a faint green wash on the walls will bring an atmosphere of classic chic here. For mature elegance, consider sage, eucalyptus, or olive against a backdrop of cream. Blue-green adds jewel interest, while a sharper acid green would suit a younger household.

kitchen

Apple green and the soft shades reminiscent of the first leaves in spring offer freshness, especially when teamed with white. Moreover, green has the power to cool the heat of the kitchen and helps to keep the cook calm when catering for a hungry crowd!

bathroom

Like blue, green also recalls the sea with its watery freshness, which makes it a very appropriate color for this room. Besides this, there is something innately hygienic and antiseptic about this color, which makes it doubly suitable here.

Living with color: Orange

As stimulating as red but far less overpowering and aggressive, orange comes in a wide range of shades, from softest peach, through coral, to cinnamon. It brings with it the fascination of the flame, the zest of the fruit and the feel of sun-baked terracotta. In the home, this extrovert color raises our spirits, encourages hospitality, and promotes conversation.

hallway

In entrances and hallways, orange gives a good first impression and never fails to offer a warm and friendly welcome. This is, after all, the color of sociability and hospitality.

bedroom

Since orange has the ability to reduce tiredness, flames and tangerines are perhaps not ideal choices for the bedroom. But there are plenty of other shades within the orange family that would suit this room. Consider peach, apricot, tawny spices, or a delicate umber wash to give this room a cozy glow.

dining room

An ideal color for this room because—like red—orange stimulates the appetite, but it does not shorten the temper, so people will leave the table satisfied and contented. In fact, orange is strongly associated with entertaining as it disperses happiness and encourages lively conversation.

living room

With the power to bring people together, any shade of orange will create a convivial ambience in rooms where the family gathers. Whether used as a main or an accent color, orange is guaranteed to bring a cheerful glow to rooms with little natural light. Also, think orange if you want to pep up an existing color scheme.

kitchen

Here, orange is a positive tonic, providing a zing to lift the heart first thing in the morning as you set about making the breakfast. If tangerine orange is too bright, go for copper and rust shades, which provide just as much warmth and vitality but which will not dazzle the eye.

bathroom

Perhaps not an obvious choice for bathrooms, where blues and greens tend to be the most popular option. Yet, with its energizing powers, orange here would certainly help to get us up and moving at the start of the day.

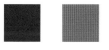

Violet

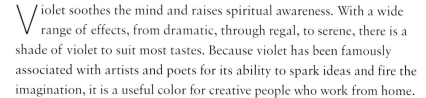

Violet soothes the mind and raises spiritual awareness. With a wide range of effects, from dramatic, through regal, to serene, there is a shade of violet to suit most tastes. Because violet has been famously associated with artists and poets for its ability to spark ideas and fire the imagination, it is a useful color for creative people who work from home.

hallway

Lilac and lavender have an enlarging effect, so are ideal in confined spaces such as corridors, where they will give the illusion of space. Purples and mauves work well if the hallway is spacious, as they will add a sense of imposing grandeur to the entrance.

bedroom

Violet brings peace and tranquility into the bedroom, and its paler shades are useful in guest rooms, where they will promote a comfortable and relaxing night's sleep. Violet is also soft and seductive: consider the sensuality of mauve velvet or purple satin.

dining room

Although the paler shades of mauve could work well as part of the color scheme here, deeper violets are best avoided—these are notorious for encouraging people to overindulge in alcohol and other addictive substances!

living room

Choose the shade of violet carefully, according to the size and location of the room. Depending on the amount of red or blue in the mix, violet can be warm or cool, can draw one in or give a feeling of space. Given the right conditions, violet will enhance a living area with its majesty and sheer sensuality.

kitchen

Although not a common choice for the kitchen, lilac and lavender in this room will bring warmth to a color scheme predominantly based on greens and blues.

bathroom

Purples and violets are well suited to the bathroom, where they lend a touch of luxury. But beware soaking in a deep tub surrounded by this color—it will encourage reflection and bring to the surface ideas from the deep unconscious.

Colors of Feng Shui

Feng Shui can create harmony and balance in the home

According to Feng Shui, the Chinese philosophy of design and placement, how we use color in our homes not only affects the atmosphere of our environment but can also actively influence our fate and fortunes. Though the rules governing this ancient art are many and complex, it is possible to filter out some of the basic principles that deal with the use of color. When applied correctly, this knowledge can bring harmony, balance, and good fortune into our lives.

The instructions regarding color are very precise and are linked to the philosophy of the five elements, which, according to the Chinese sages, underpin the physical universe. Each element represents a set of qualities that all interrelate with one another. Seasons, compass directions, physical shapes, parts of the body, and, of course, colors, are just some of the components that form part of each elemental group.

Elements and directions

According to the rules of Feng Shui, each element, and so each color, is linked to a particular compass direction. From this are formed the fundamental rules for using color in interior design. Use the compass shown opposite and the chart on pages 48–49 to identify which colors will work best for specific areas of your home.

For example, you may find that your living room faces east. Introducing the color green and wooden objects into the eastern sector of your home would be in harmony with the elemental forces governing this area. Since east is associated with family, relationships, and health, these areas of your life, in particular, may be improved by making the appropriate changes.

Getting the elements and their colors into the right locations will also go a long way toward attracting good *chi*—the energy known as the "cosmic breath," which brings benefits and blessings into our lives.

Putting the principles into practice

If you do not have a compass to find the true orientation of your home, you could make a good stab at it by noting where the sun rises and sets to give you the east and west bearings. If you are using a compass, stand in the center of your house, or room and note the directions.

Now, take a large sheet of paper and draw a floor plan of your property, marking in the room divisions. If you have only one room, simply draw the outline of the floor area.

Mark the compass directions on your plan, indicating the four main cardinal points of south, east, north, and west, as well as the midpoints of southeast, southwest, northeast and northwest. Note which rooms, or areas of a room, lie in each of these eight directions.

Many rooms and houses have an irregular outline. Perhaps your apartment or one of your rooms is L-shaped, in which case there will be a missing sector. Feng Shui offers specific guidelines for dealing with these missing

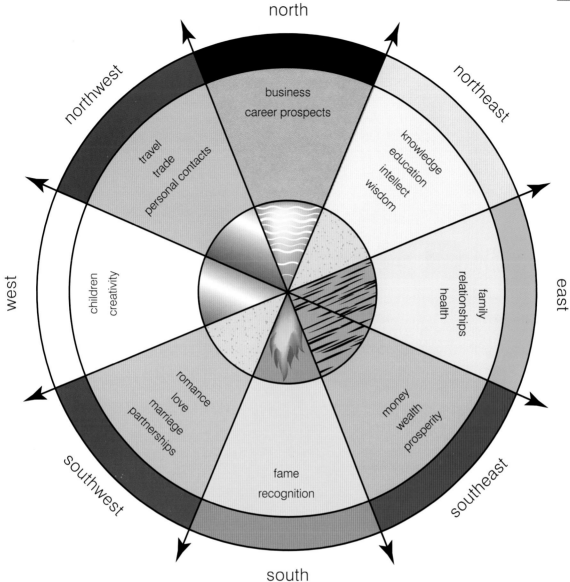

corners. Hanging a large mirror on the wall that looks over the missing space will give an optical illusion that "recreates" or "fills in" that area. Alternatively, if the missing space is part of the garden, treat that as part of the sector and fill it with urns, water features or flowers in the colors appropriate to that section.

The eight directions each represent different facets of your life—career, children, love, money, and so on, as described in the chart above.

Irrespective of which rooms or areas line up with your compass directions, applying a few of the suggestions recommended by Feng Shui may produce some surprising, if not dramatic, results. If your relationships have hit a rocky patch, if more money goes out than comes in, if your children are argumentative, or if you feel you are always missing out on promotion, making a few of these modifications could well change your prospects forever.

	north	northeast	east	southeast
represents	business career prospects	knowledge education study intellect wisdom	family relationships health and well-being of members of your household	money wealth prosperity
auspicious colors				
element	water	earth	wood	wood
accessorize with	black and white checkerboard prints, blue- and-white-striped pillows, large metal-framed mirror	sunflowers and marigolds, tiles in vivid hues of paprika, saffron, and cayenne	a pine dresser containing blue china, crystal glasses, decanters and vases, black lacquer cabinet black ash furniture	paintings of rivers and waterfalls, dark blue rug, arrangement of indoor plants, preferably with round leaves
for good luck	a fish tank with eight gold and one black fish, metal wind chimes brass wall plaques	crystals, amethyst geodes, pretty pebbles in a bowl glass paperweight ceramic urns porcelain figurines	round-leafed plants (such as a jade plant on a wooden plantstand), pictures of your family	water feature, aquarium with two gold and one black fish, ornaments in polished wood
avoid	red, green, beige, and brown earthenware pots plants wooden furniture	green and black, metal trunks, wooden tables and chairs, trees, bushes, indoor plants	red or white paintwork metal cabinets silver or brass objects	metallic picture frames, pots, pans, knives, and other sharp kitchen objects

	south	southwest	west	northwest
represents	fame and recognition in the world	partnerships marriage romance love	children, their fate and fortunes creative projects and powers	new beginnings international trade travel mentors useful contacts
auspicious colors				
element	fire	earth	metal	metal
accessorize with	jungle prints with hot, bright shades of red and green	sun-baked tones of cinnamon, and spice-colored accessories with earthy Aztec designs, work well in this sector	golden yellow patterned throws, white muslin draperies with polished brass tiebacks	fabrics in mellow shades of nutmeg and ochre, marble tiles
for good luck	lamps, uplights, open fires, red candles, tall wooden candlesticks	ceramic pots, a pair of china ducks, pictures of happy couples – display objects in pairs to represent twosomes and togetherness	a bronze statuette, pottery, vases, urns, electrical appliances, stereos and television sets	place or hang a gold or brass bell tied with a red ribbon here, metal wind chimes
avoid	blue, black, or white, any type of water feature—as this symbolically puts out the fire and douses your good reputation	blue, black or water, which will symbolically put out the fire of passion and romance. Also avoid wooden chests or furniture here	red, green, brown water features, open fires, candles	greens, browns open fires and stoves in this location if the kitchen is sited here

Color at work

Color used in the workplace visually sets the tone and reflects the image of a company. The right color scheme can make a dramatic difference to the workforce. By introducing light, warmth, and energy into a building, color can change the mood, atmosphere, and perspective and contribute to the comfort and well-being of worker and client alike.

Creating workspace

In a study carried out by psychologists, subjects were shown a series of identically-sized rooms, each painted a different color. The subjects judged that the darker-colored rooms felt considerably more crowded than those painted in lighter tones. It was the intensity of the colors that proved the significant factor. A room painted light green, for example, was perceived as less crowded than its darker green counterpart, though in reality both were exactly the same size and equally populated.

This shows that, where space is at a premium or where offices are shared, a coat of paint in a warm, low-intensity color will give a valuable sense of space and a greater feeling of comfort.

The décor of the workplace has another significant contribution to make. Color affects us subliminally, so it has a subtle impact on morale and can impair or enhance a worker's performance. This was demonstrated in a factory where high absenteeism was creating a serious problem. The cause was found to lie in the factory's harsh blue lighting, which was having an adverse affect on the workers, making them look pale and draining them of energy. Stripping out the lighting and replacing it with a warm beige light solved the problem and reduced absenteeism to normal levels.

Setting the mood

The color scheme employed in the workplace should also be appropriate to the nature of the work carried out within those walls. Garish colors would not be suitable in an environment where formality or decorum are required. Conversely, dull, dingy colors would be inappropriate where the employees are expected to generate exciting and creative ideas.

Whether we consciously recognize it or not, color subtly communicates the nature and ethos of a company. Striking the right tone can make all the difference between boom and bust.

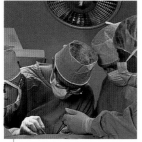

The soothing, therapeutic nature of green makes it an ideal color for the stressful conditions of the surgical environment.

Red is ideal for places where brisk social exchanges take place, such as hallways and restaurants. The energizing qualities of red lend themselves especially well to clubs and dance halls. Red is useful, too, as a bold accent color in workshops and activity areas, where movement and speed of production are required. However, since this is not a restful color, it should be avoided in offices and used sparingly in doctors' waiting rooms, hospitals, and clinics. Red speeds our perception of time passing, so this is a useful color for restaurants and fast-food outlets, where a brisk through-trade is important to business.

Orange enlivens the atmosphere, gets people moving and makes them feel good. It therefore comes into its own in the gym, dance hall, or theater workshop, while orange décor in reception areas offers a pleasant welcome. Tests have shown that orange has the power to boost memory and learning, so it can be put to good use in lecture halls or classrooms, and especially around the chalkboard, to facilitate the easier absorption of facts and data. Because orange has proved beneficial in stimulating sales, it can be used successfully in shops and retail outlets.

Yellow is associated with the intellect, so is an ideal color for offices, especially those set up at home. Since it stimulates the reasoning processes and encourages balanced judgment, warm yellow tones would especially suit lawyers' offices. Activities involving public relations, advertising, and design also benefit from this color.

Green has a soothing, restful reputation, although too much can give off a sense of inertia. This is a color that needs to be used with care in offices and workshops. Since it encourages discernment and balanced judgement, green is an admirable color in courtrooms, legal offices, or departments of social welfare. The healing properties of this color can be put to good effect in most medical or therapeutic environments, such as hospitals. Green is particularly well-suited to operating rooms.

Blue is an excellent choice for libraries, bookstores and publishing houses, as it encourages ease of communication and clarity of thought. It stimulates the intellect, promotes concentration, and fosters an atmosphere of peace and quiet. Its formality makes it suitable for public-sector offices or for civic and financial institutions. In a blue room, we feel that time goes by slowly. This feature may be used to advantage in high-pressure environments, such as newspaper offices, where working to tight deadlines is common.

Violet has a sense of reverence which makes it ideal for use in churches, and other places of worship. Its lighter shades, which are feminine and creative, suit artistic and creative environments, such as drama and music schools.

Magenta has the same spiritual qualities as purple and is used to great effect in chapels and cathedrals. Lecture halls, too, benefit from the awe-inspiring attributes of this color, as do large, imposing entrances with high or vaulted ceilings.

The Color Insight Cards

Colors act as a mirror to our psyche and emotions

Have you noticed how some mornings you wake up in a "blue" mood and you pick out a navy outfit to wear for the day? The very next morning, you might decide that blue is dull and you are drawn instead to a chic beige ensemble, a bright red suit, or smart green pants.

It is well known that we respond to different colors according to our moods. The colors that attract at any given moment in time reflect those feelings and give us an instant insight into our state of mind.

As you shuffle your Color Insight Cards prior to laying them out, keep your eyes shut, your mind clear, and your breathing deep and even.

Using the cards

1. *Slowly shuffle the twelve Color Insight Cards,* your eyes and letting your mind go blank. Breathe in slowly to the count of seven, hold for four, then breathe out to the count of seven. Repeat three times, taking each breath deep into your abdomen, and shuffling the cards all the while.

2. *When you feel ready, lay the cards out at random in front of you.*

3. *Look at the display and choose the color that attracts you the most. Try not to pick a color because it is the one that matches your décor or because it teams with your wardrobe. Choose instinctively. Go with your gut reaction, even if you are drawn to a color you might not normally choose.*

4. *Pick out your first choice and place it face down to one side. Now, choose a second card in the same way. Place it upside down on top of your first choice. Repeat once more with a third choice.*

5. *Choose the color you like least; the one that spontaneously turns you off. Pick up that card and place it to one side.*

6. *Remove the remaining eight cards. Place your first, second, and third choices in a row to your left and your fourth choice a little apart on the right.*

Tap into your subconscious

The cards are designed to enable you to tap into your subconscious and unravel your innermost thoughts and needs. Whether you have a problem, feel confused, or want to understand more about your inner self, use the cards to focus on your present situation and find out what your color choices say about you. The color insight test described opposite can be repeated as often as every day, if you like, to monitor changes going on in your life.

Using the Color Insight Cards

The Color Insight pack consists of twelve colored cards: pink, red, yellow, green, blue, turquoise, violet, magenta, brown, black, gray, and white. Each has been selected for its associated symbolic meaning. The test is simple to do; follow the six steps opposite, then discover what your choices mean below and on the following pages.

Analyze your choice

Your first three choices will mirror your current thoughts and feelings. The fourth will reveal something you may be avoiding.

∘ The first color tells you about the frame of mind you are in. It describes your moods and emotions and reveals how these will "color" your behaviour.

∘ Your second color choice tells you about the plans you have in your mind and how you are likely to act and react, whether consciously or subconsciously, in order to bring those plans to life.

∘ The third choice of color throws light on your present circumstances. It hints at how you have arrived at this point and suggests what else is happening in your life that might be influencing your current thoughts and emotions.

∘ Your last choice—that is, the color you like least—is as important as your other three choices because it gives clues as to what you might be avoiding or ignoring at the moment. Perhaps it is a physical situation you wish to avoid. Or it might be a quality in yourself you are suppressing. Or something that is going on in your life that you do not wish to recognize. Here, the exercise asks you to consider this area and to decide whether addressing it would help to balance your situation.

Discover what your choices reveal about you on the following pages.

Finding the balance

Once you have chosen your Color Insight Cards, find ways of bringing those colors into your life on that day. Wearing clothes of your chosen favorites is an obvious way to do this. But you could also carry a book or a folder in those colors. Or you could stand your Color Cards on your desk or worktop.

Another alternative might be to actually eat your colors —bananas, oranges, tomatoes, cabbage, or eggplants —or drink solarized water. (You can find more information about colored foods and solarized water on pages 100–101.) However, don't forget to introduce your fourth color choice, too. It is vitally important to incorporate this color, even if only in a tiny amount, in order to achieve a true balance of your thoughts and feelings.

Your Color Insight Card selections

1. Pink

as your first choice

You are in a pleasant frame of mind and satisfied with your situation at present. Pink as a first choice is often the sign of a well-balanced personality. An affectionate and playful nature makes you a lovable individual, sometimes shy and sensitive, but you bounce back after a setback.

as your second choice

Your patience, tolerance, and adaptability mean that you find it easy to compromise. In fact, your natural inclination is to avoid arguments. With your compliant manner, you find that people respond favorably to you.

as your third choice

You have achieved at least some of your ideals and feel settled and secure. Your creative and emotional needs have been met, and it pleases you to think that you have the ability to resolve issues practically and with good common sense.

as your last choice

Do you have a tendency to make life difficult for yourself? Perhaps you find it hard to compromise, to be of service to others, or to give unconditional love. If this is so, and if it is adversely affecting your relationships, try carrying a piece of rose quartz (see page 84) or placing a chunk of it on your desk.

2. Red

as your first choice

You are full of energy, vitality, and excitement. Your passions are roused and you are in the mood for adventure. This choice shows that you are ready to take the lead and you mean business.

as your second choice

Your actions and reactions are impulsive and spontaneous. Though you are more prone than usual to taking risks or making decisions on the spur of the moment, you are determined to succeed, and your dynamic energy will ensure that you put one hundred percent effort into whatever you decide to undertake.

as your third choice

Exciting developments—a new romance, a creative project, or the achievement of an ambition—are behind your feelings of success and zest for life.

as your last choice

Enthusiasm, confidence, and vitality are at a low ebb. Perhaps you are running away from a challenge or feeling that you can't assert yourself. It may be that a buildup of pressure or a humdrum routine have taken their toll and depleted your energies. If so, consider taking a break or even just a few early nights. Rekindle your drive by sitting under a red light or by wearing red clothes.

3. Yellow

as your first choice

Bright, alert, and cheerful, you have a positive attitude and are prepared to meet others halfway. With your buoyant and optimistic outlook, you breeze through life, ever excited by the prospect of new situations and people to stimulate you.

as your second choice

Socially skilled, and a gifted communicator, you approach your work with clarity of thought and win others around with your powers of persuasion. Monotony is your biggest fear, so variety is essential for you. You enjoy multitasking, but beware not to take on more than you can handle.

as your third choice

A new interest has attracted your attention, and you are thoroughly enjoying pitting your wits against the challenges it is presenting.

as your last choice

Past disappointments have made you wary of others and considerably dented your confidence and self-esteem. There is a danger you might withdraw inside yourself or lose contact with your circle of friends and acquaintances. Regain your sense of self by wearing an item of yellow clothing, carrying a citrine (see page 85), or doing the task accentuation exercise (see page 91).

4. Green

as your first choice

You are calm and collected. You feel strong and at peace with yourself and with the world around you. You recognize that you will achieve your aims by adopting a fair-minded attitude and working steadily and consistently.

as your second choice

You are seeking to improve matters, find logical solutions, heal rifts, clear up anomalies, and generally clean up your act.

as your third choice

Your circumstances are offering you the "green light" to go ahead with your plans.

as your last choice

Ask yourself whether you are taking a biased view of your situation at the moment. Green as your least preferred choice suggests a shift of emphasis. Perhaps you feel that there are barriers in your way. Have these been erected by other people, or are they of your own making? Try to take a more detached view in order to see the whole picture. You need to be more grounded, which, in turn, should help you to find a practical solution. Try the Call to the Sun exercise (see pages 94–95) for grounding and inspiration.

5. Blue

as your first choice

With cool logic and an analytical disposition, you keep your emotions under control. Your feelings are balanced, your integrity intact, and your judgment unbiased. Tranquil in mind and heart, you are calm and concerned with inner thoughts.

as your second choice

Eager to do the right thing, you come across as dependable and trustworthy. You are resourceful, well organized, and able to give your full concentration to any task. Some people may initially misinterpret your formality as aloofness, but your honesty, and disarming willingness to cooperate with others, soon wins them around.

as your third choice

People have come to rely upon you, to recognize your loyalty and to listen to your wisdom. You have a mature outlook on life and are satisfied that you can usually find innovative solutions to problems.

as your last choice

Restlessness could be the cause of any malaise you may be feeling. What about dissatisfaction in your life? Are you feeling overburdened with responsibility, unfulfilled by your relationships, or bored with your present situation? Try to think rationally about your circumstances. If you are also finding it difficult to concentrate or to understand your emotions, try Aura-Soma therapy.

6. Turquoise

as your first choice

Easy in mind and heart, you are feeling calm and relaxed. There is a mystical element to your mood that radiates inner spirituality. You are sensitive to those around you and are able to tune in to their thoughts. Your powers of self-expression are good, and, whatever your age, you feel young at heart.

as your second choice

Essentially altruistic, you go out of your way to help other people. Connecting with others is important to your well-being, which means that you function best when you are working as part of a team. But it is in a close, intimate relationship that your true creativity comes alive and your talents flourish.

as your third choice

Events have brought out your emotional strengths, showing you have the power to withstand external pressures and remain true to your principles. This has given you great confidence, and you are now convinced that you are in control of your own fate.

as your last choice

A feeling of rejection or isolation, or an inability to get on the same wavelength as your companions, often accompanies this choice. How do you come across to others? Are you getting your message across? If not, others may see you as stubborn or unhelpful. If so, try to work on your aura and practice radiating loving vibrations (see page 69).

7. Violet

as your first choice

Imaginative and inspired, you are something of a visionary. But, like all seers, you may find yourself in two minds—your feet on the ground but your head in the clouds. Despite these conflicts, you are serene and sophisticated, and blessed with much creative talent.

as your second choice

You are guided by intuition and a strong sense of aesthetics. So you are forward-thinking and tackle everything with flair. You come across as charming and open-minded, full of ideas and dreams. Extremely sensitive, you seek a soul-union with a partner who will heal your emotional insecurity.

as your third choice

You are inclined to look at life through rose-colored spectacles and to create fantasies in your mind. In a creative occupation, these are valuable skills. But on a practical level, this may have led to unrealistic expectations and disappointments.

as your last choice

You have worked hard to become mature and to let go of childish habits. You see yourself as a realistic individual who is leading a responsible adult life. But could it be that such a sensible approach leaves little room for fun, spontaneity, or childlike wonder? Try the Call to the Sun exercise (see page 94), and it may open you to all sorts of possibilities.

8. Magenta

as your first choice

Open and forthright, you are clear-sighted and prefer to take a direct approach. Given to inspirational thoughts, you learned a long time ago that following your intuition never leads you astray. You are emotionally stable, but you may be prone to self-importance now and then.

as your second choice

Have you noticed a change—how you have become weary of superficiality and are seeking a greater depth of understanding? Your views are now your own: more powerful and committed. With your new-found self-assurance you are no longer prepared to blindly accept the beliefs of others.

as your third choice

Whether physically, emotionally, or psychologically, you have been busy "cleaning up your act". You have let go of patterns of behavior that have been blocking your progress and pruned away emotional dead wood. Now you are free to move on.

as your last choice

Perhaps simply because of a lack of energy, you hang on to ideas, attitudes, memories, or emotions that are past their sell-by dates. You are practical and like to feel your feet on terra firma. You may be well grounded, but consider also whether you need to connect with the spiritual side of your nature; try using a pomander (see pages 112–117) daily.

as your first choice

Practical, logical, and down-to-earth, you are famed for your good sense and pragmatic approach to life. You are steady and consistent, liking to go at your own pace and hating to be rushed. A settled existence is important. Personal safety, strong roots, and a happy home life are what you seek.

as your second choice

Never one to act impulsively, you like to take time to consider your options. Material security and physical well-being are crucial to your happiness. You are prepared to work long and hard in order to amass the creature comforts you require.

as your third choice

Have you been worried about health issues recently? Perhaps an illness has taught you the value of good health and how important it is to make the most of every minute of the day. If so, this is a lesson well learned.

as your last choice

There is a danger that you push yourself too hard, and you need to take more time to consider your health and physical well-being. Ask yourself whether you get enough exercise, quality sleep, and a balanced diet. Now is the time to start thinking about a new fitness or relaxation regime. Meditation would also be advantageous.

10. Black

as your first choice

This is an unusual first choice and shows that you prize your independence and individuality. It is often selected by someone who feels a need to rebel against the norm and to do his or her own thing. Stubbornness is a characteristic, suggesting a refusal to compromise.

as your second choice

You have very definite aims and will not let anything stand in the way of achieving your objectives. You like the idea of shrouding yourself in mystery so that you come across as enigmatic. If you are confronted with opposition of any kind, you are likely to respond by digging in your heels.

as your third choice

Rejection may have played a role in your current circumstances. Either you have had experience of being spurned or else you have been the one to turn your back on someone or something that has been constricting you in your life. Either way, you have made your choices and drawn a line between the past and the actions you will take in the future.

as your last choice

With your well-balanced attitude and outlook on life, you have the reins of your destiny firmly in your own hands. Try the Call to the Sun exercise (see pages 94–95) to check that you are definitely following your chosen path.

11. Gray

as your first choice

As a neutral color, this choice reveals that you are a "middle-of-the-road" person, someone who refuses to take sides. You go through life avoiding commitment. Perhaps you see this as a way of protecting yourself, of not getting involved.

as your second choice

In your desire to avoid confrontation, you come across as indecisive. This uncertainty tends to both limit your options and narrow your scope of vision.

as your third choice

Involvement has proved onerous and taken its physical, mental, and emotional toll. You have experienced the stressful situation of being pulled one way and pushed the other. Amid this conflict, you have sought to find a balance as a way of extricating yourself from the problem.

as your last choice

Never one to brood or to look at the bleak side of life, you throw yourself heart and soul into whatever you undertake. Sitting on the fence is not your style, and because you want to be part of everything that is going on, you tend to take on too much and over-commit your time and energies. Take a look at the Aura-Soma pomanders (see page 112), and use them to strengthen your aura, so that your energies can be channeled constructively.

12. White

as your first choice

This selection means you take a youthful attitude to life. Perhaps there is a touch of the Peter Pan in your nature—a desire never to grow up but to see the world with childlike wonder. On the one hand, this attitude will keep you young at heart. However, its innocence may be at the expense of the rich fulfillment that truly mature experiences can bring.

as your second choice

With clarity of vision, your ideas are original and you want to put your creativity into practice. You have both confidence and courage on your side and are well equipped to take on whatever the situation demands.

as your third choice

A desire for new beginnings has given you the confidence to step out into the unknown. Now you feel strong, independent, and sure of the direction you want your life to take.

as your last choice

Consider whether your life is anything but simple. Perhaps you move from one complicated situation to another, picking your way through physical, psychological, and emotional clutter of one sort or another. If so, start now to delegate and have a good old clear-out—in every sense of the word. Cultivate serenity and simplicity by visualizing white light entering your system and cleansing your life.

Part two

The healing power of color

Color and Nature can be used to balance mind, body, and spirit

There is an undeniable health-giving quality to color. When the sun shines, colors around us intensify, and our spirits come alive. Since ancient times, the healing properties of light, of which color is a part, have been recognized and incorporated into therapies specifically designed to balance and tone the mind, body, and spirit. Essentially gentle and uplifting, many of these therapies can be practiced in the comfort and privacy of our own homes. Whether through visualization, through understanding the aura and chakra system, through physical interaction with Nature, or through the use of crystals and gemstones, color in all its forms and glories can help to rejuvenate our energies and bring us tranquility and peace of mind.

Introducing color healing

Healing with
color is an
ancient art

There is much to suggest that the healing benefits of color may have been known to civilizations as old as the Sumerians—around 3000 B.C.E.—and maybe even long before that. Certainly, texts dating back to around 1550 B.C.E. reveal that the ancient Egyptians not only used color routinely as a therapeutic tool, but also developed this art to extremely high levels of efficacy.

An ancient healing art

At the time of the pharaohs, healing temples (perhaps the equivalent of our modern-day hospitals) were constructed. These incorporated quartz crystal screens which acted like prisms, splitting light into its component colors. These crystals directed individual colors into separate chambers, where patients were placed according to their ailments. Those who were low in energy, for example, might be revitalized in chambers flooded with red light rays, while others needing to be tranquilized might have been placed in rooms that were bathed in blue light.

Harnessing color energies

What was recognized all that time ago is that the organs in the body each vibrate at different frequencies. A perfectly healthy body will be "in tune"— rather like an engine—with the vibrations of its various parts, synchronized so that the whole system works in complete harmony. Stress, strain, or emotional trauma, however, will throw those vibrations out of sync, and as the system becomes imbalanced, ill-health follows.

Healers who work with color maintain that because colors are part of light, they are a source of energy. Each color, they observe, is carried on a different frequency, and each one matches perfectly the frequency of one or other of the organs in the body.

According to color therapy, when one of our organs is out of balance, it is possible to "retune" it by absorbing into our bodies the energy of its corresponding color. These vibrations will nudge the affected organ back into its correct frequency again.

Determining which color is required, where the body's energies are out of kilter, and how to apply the precise color to correct the imbalances is central to the art of color therapy. Since color healing is an ancient art, a considerable amount is now known about colors and how they correspond to the body. From this knowledge we can identify which illnesses respond to or benefit from exposure to specific colors.

Understanding the aura and chakra systems is one of the first steps on the way to detecting where the body's energies are out of balance. Once these imbalances have been pinpointed, a healer will choose which of the color therapies is most suitable to treat them. Some of the most popular types of color healing are listed below. These are examined in further detail on the following pages.

Types of color therapy

- *Crystals and visualization, though subtle, can prove powerful color healing tools.*

- *Some healers project colored light rays onto the affected area, either from a lamp or from the healers' hands.*

- *Wearing the required color as part of clothing not only helps psychologically but also enables us to absorb color physically.*

- *A walk in the garden is often a tonic, because, apart from the fresh air and exercise, it exposes us to the colors of Nature, which we take into our bodies through our eyes.*

- *Color can be effectively absorbed through the skin using Aura-Soma oils, which are based on a holistic recipe that combines gem essences, oils, and fragrances with colors of jewel-like intensity. Just looking at the bottles of vibrant color can be enough to lift the spirits.*

- *Simple as it may sound, eating richly colored foods or drinking water that has been solarized (see page 101) has been known to have a positive therapeutic effect.*

Light passing through a stained glass window forms an awe-inspiring mosaic of color and is used in churches to exalt the spirits of the congregation.

Color in physical diagnosis

Color can be used to diagnose disease

During the first century B.C.E., the Persian philosopher and physician Avicenna wrote a definitive treatise on medicine. Not only was this the most influential reference book on the subject of its age, but it set the standard in medicinal practice for centuries to come. It was here, in his *Canon Medicinae*, that Avicenna put forward his observations on the changes of color in the body and their correspondence to ill health. Giving detailed examples, he went on to demonstrate how physicians could use body color as a guide to diagnose specific diseases.

Eye color

According to the complementary therapy of iridology, the eyes—and especially the irises—offer a rich source of diagnostic clues to disease. To detect ill health, the iris is mapped out like a clock face: the skin, tissues, organs, and muscles are represented at specific locations around the disk.

○ White lines, brown flecks, and yellow patches all pinpoint weaknesses, illness, or trauma in the body areas that correspond to where these markings occur.

Hand and nail color

To hand analysts, the hand is a powerful diagnostic tool. The color of the palms and nail beds give valuable clues to both the character and health of the individual in question.

○ White hands denote a lackluster personality, together with lowered energy levels and poor vitality.

○ Yellow or white nail beds have a variety of causes, ranging from liver dysfunction, jaundice, anemia, venereal disease, and to an excess of beta-carotene in the system.

○ Blue tinges to the fingers, other than those temporarily caused by cold weather, suggest possible respiratory disorders or cardiovascular problems. The same applies to any blue discoloration of the nail beds, and particularly so of the moons.

○ White spots or flecks in the nail are associated with mineral imbalances and nutritional deficiencies. Mineral poisoning, bacterial infections, and organic diseases also stamp their characteristic color markings into the nail.

To this day, clinical science recognizes the link between color and disease, and doctors take into account color in the body when making their diagnoses. Certain parts of the body can yield useful information. Noticeable changes in skin pigmentation, particularly of the lips and nail beds and around the eyes, and in some cases even changes in the color of feces and urine, can yield valuable clues to support their medical findings.

Skin color

Changes in skin color often indicate a person's health. Any draining away of the normal healthy pink or brown tones of the skin tends to suggest conditions that have a weakening effect on the body.

- Pallor is a manifestation of shock. Paling of the skin can also be a sign of iron deficiency and is particularly evident on the inside of the eyelids, which lose their vital red tones in cases of anemia.

- Yellowing of the skin, most pronounced in the sclera—the normally white part—of the eye, is an immediate sign of jaundice or liver dysfunction.

- A grayish darkening of the skin around the eyes may indicate problems with the kidneys.

- A blue tinge to the skin or lips indicates a shortage of oxygen. This can be caused by lung diseases and coronary problems, and is also found in cases of gas poisoning.

- Blushing is a sign of embarrassment, but persistent redness can denote circulatory problems.

Tongue color

The color of the tongue is minutely studied in certain Eastern therapies such as Ayurveda, whose practitioners see a correspondence between changes in patches of color on the tongue and impending ill health. According to this ancient art, the tongue may be read like a map of the body, in a similar manner as with the ear or the foot in reflexology.

- The tip of the tongue relates to the heart. If this area is too red, it may imply a fault in the cardiac or circulatory rhythms.

- Excessive red patches in the center of the tongue point to problems of the liver; a similar patch farther back denotes that kidney function is out of kilter.

- Yellowness of the tongue suggests that the intestines are not working as well as they should.

- Purple indicates that the circulation is sluggish

- A pale, whitish tongue implies a general weakness and possible iron deficiency.

The aura

All living things emit a certain amount of electricity, which surrounds the body in an electromagnetic field known as the aura. This field forms itself into a ring of radiant light around the outside of the physical body, and, though invisible to most eyes, it is made up of many colors. Each color symbolizes a specific organ, a psychological characteristic, or a physical condition, and so describes the moods, feelings, disposition, or state of health of the individual. Golden haloes painted around the heads of deities and saints are depictions of the aura—gold being the highest expression of spirituality and divinity.

Here, a butterfly reveals a strong and healthy auric field of color around its delicate body. The colors of the aura can be used to gauge emotional and physical health.

into our auras will be vibrant and bright, and the emanations will project far beyond the outline of our physical bodies.

However, when we are ill or unhappy, our energies are lessened, and so our auric rings may become punctured or indented, or the vibrancy of their colors may diminish. Dark, murky spots in the aura, for example, may reflect hidden anger, disharmony, negative emotions, or blocked energy which, if left unresolved, could potentially lead to disease.

Healers, whether by sight or through intuitive sensation, are able to detect the condition of a person's aura and can help to put right suspected problems by transmitting energies through their own bodies to the individual they are treating. By running their hands around a sick person's body, the healer is able to "feel" where the energy in the aura is low. Then, by concentrating and transmitting the appropriate color to those

The size of the auric ring, how far it extends outward, the number of different colors it contains, as well as the tone, quality, and intensity of those colors, are all very significant. When we are confident, contented, physically fit, and enjoying good health, the energy we give out is strong. Therefore, the colors we radiate

weak spots, the healer is able to shore up the force of that person's auric field. Think of it as jump-starting someone else's battery with your own.

Making the aura visible

Paintings and writings from ancient times suggest that civilizations throughout history have recognized the existence of the aura. Though only comparatively few people can actually see the colored radiations with their own eyes, special techniques developed at the beginning of the twentieth century now make it possible for anyone to observe the spectacular beauty of these auric rays.

Kilner's screen

It was in the closing years of the nineteenth century that Walter Kilner, a physician working in a London hospital, became interested in the body's electromagnetic energy. This was at a time when Roentgen was developing the X-ray and when new discoveries involving diagnostic techniques were pushing back the boundaries of medical understanding.

Through his research, Kilner came to believe that the condition of the electrical field that envelops the human body could be used to detect potential illness, and he invented a special lens through which the field—or aura—could be viewed. The lens, made of sheets of glass painted with a special dye, became known as the "dicyanin screen", and using this did indeed allow the aura to become visible.

With practice, Kilner began to observe that dull patches in the aura tended to concentrate around the organs or body areas that had been injured or that were diseased. By repeated viewing, he was also able to observe that after successful treatment, these patches disappeared and the normal color of the aura returned to the individual.

Despite his efforts, however, Kilner's work was not well received by the more orthodox clinicians of his day, and the subsequent outbreak of the First World War finally put a stop to his further research in this area.

Kirlian photography

Some forty years later and many thousands of miles away, a Russian electrical engineer named Semyon Kirlian was inspired by a process of electrotherapy treatment that he happened to observe on a visit to a hospital. He noticed that when the treatment was administered, tiny flashes of light were seen sparking off the skin.

Kirlian believed that these electrical sparks could somehow prove valuable to both medicine and science, and, together with his wife, he set about devising a method of photographing them. His work resulted in the development of Kirlian photography, a technique that captures the shape and colors of the aura on film.

By the 1960s, Kirlian was able to demonstrate that health and disease are reflected in the condition and brilliance of the vibrational color ring that surrounds all physical bodies. Moreover, by using before-and-after photographs, he even went so far as to establish that significant changes occur in the auric ring long before a breakdown in health occurs, and that both the shape and color of the ring return to normal after successful treatment has taken place.

Learning to see the aura

There are many benefits to seeing the aura. Not only does it enable us to detect low-energy spots and potential ill health, but it also gives us instant and valuable psychological insights into a person's character and disposition. However, the ability to see the aura with the physical eye is rare, and only a few gifted individuals can do this naturally. But, as with many skills, it can be learned.

You may have to try several times before getting any result. But do persist; it is well worth the effort. You could take it in turns with the other sitter, which is especially effective if this is a friend or partner.

> The aura can give valuable insights into character and disposition

How to see the aura

1. You will need to sit in a room that is not too brightly lit. Dimmed natural or full-spectrum light is best, perhaps with the draperies or blinds partially drawn. Avoid a room with direct sunlight.

2. Ask the person whose aura you want to view, to sit with his or her back to a wall, about 3–4 in. (8–10 cm) away from it. A plain, preferably dark-colored, wall is ideal. If there are no plain, dark walls, drape a cloth over a bookcase, shelf unit, or door behind the seated person. If you are using a drape, smooth the cloth as best you can, because folds and wrinkles can distort the image.

3. Sit yourself directly opposite the person, several feet away. Arrange the room so that you are sitting with the light behind you, with your back to the window, perhaps, or with a low-wattage lamp behind you.

4. As you both sit quietly and still, begin to breathe slowly and rhythmically, taking each breath down deep into the abdomen. Feel the tension ease away, drop your shoulders, and relax your muscles.

5. Now, cast your gaze to the person opposite you. Do not look directly at him or her. The trick is to de-focus your eyes and look beyond or through the person.

6. If you need to, close your eyes to give them a little rest every so often and then try again. Some people find that looking through half-closed eyes is more successful, so try that if you are having no luck at first.

Layers of color

Eventually, with practice, things start to happen. To begin with, you may start to see a narrow, grayish-white or blue band around the person you're observing. This is the physical auric body, the innermost ring of the aura. Later, you will start to make out another ring surrounding the first one, and then—somewhat like the Russian babushka dolls inside a doll—you will be able to identify more and more layers of rings beyond. The whole envelope of rings can extend about 1½ ft (½ m), sometimes less and sometimes much more.

Soon you will be able to distinguish the colors carried on fine rays of light as subtle and luminescent as a rainbow. The predominance of particular colors, plus their brightness and

extent, will reveal much about the person you are observing. You can find out what each of the colors represent on pages 70–71.

Personal space

We each have a personal space: an area around our own body that we define as our physical and psychological boundary. Whether we are tall or short, well-padded or thin as a rake, the size of the personal space we create for ourselves contributes to our "stature" or our importance in the eyes of other people.

Royal personages, world leaders, and other famous celebrities, for example, tend to create a comparatively large personal space around themselves. So do extroverts, who need room for their wide-flung, expansive gestures. Introverts, on the other hand, tend to withdraw inside themselves, hugging their personal spaces close to their own bodies.

Maintaining our personal space, which may be likened to a bubble that surrounds us and into which our auras flow, is important to our comfort and well-being. A stranger or an aggressive individual coming too close and effectively invading our space makes us feel threatened and uncomfortable, and we instinctively draw away. Lovers, however, willingly allow their personal spaces to be breached by the beloved, and, as they happily invite their partners in, so their two auras meet and fuse into one.

the aura can give insights into:

- *physical state of health*
- *personality traits*
- *mentality*
- *emotions*
- *spiritual development*
- *intellectual strengths*
- *psychological weaknesses*
- *energy blockages*
- *intentions and motivation*
- *truthfulness*
- *trustworthiness*

The colors of the aura

Our hopes and dreams, our moods and feelings, our anxieties and fears, our characters and personalities, our mentality and our health are all reflected by the colors that we radiate into our auras. A white aura encompasses all the colors of the spectrum, and its vibrancy expresses vitality and well-being. Each color tells a story of its own. A predominance of a particular color or a sudden flare shooting through a person's aura will reveal a great deal about that individual.

red

This color indicates ambition and drive. As might be expected, red is found emanating from dynamic individuals; people with masses of passion and energy.

Red shows up in the aura of an individual who possesses a healthy libido and strong sexual power. It shows excitement. Pinks and lighter shades of red reflect a loving nature and a romantic turn of mind. Dark red can reveal anger, jealousy and violent intent—the greater the amount of deep red in the aura, the more aggressive the personality.

Everyone's aura is different; the balance of colors varies from person to person, indicating certain characteristics or personality traits.

orange

A bouncy, progressive auric color, orange denotes vital energy and a warm, outgoing nature. Those with a concentration of this color in their aura will display good sense, a keen intellect, and a good-natured attitude to all those with whom they come into contact.

By contrast, a dull, murky orange in the aura warns of vanity and egocentricity.

yellow

A lively intelligence and a happy disposition are revealed in a yellow aura. Yellow also shows the ability to concentrate on a task and work logically. A dull, mustard shade indicates a possessive character.

Gold in the vibrations is very special because it is the color of goodness. A completely golden aura is rare and found only around those who are highly evolved or devout.

green

This color is associated with kindness and a talent for healing. Deeper shades, though, can denote a tendency to insincerity and deception.

Light green indicates a sympathetic, intuitive and sensitive nature. Blue-green or turquoise is a strong color in the aura, suggesting an energetic nature.

Too much green in the aura can denote aloofness and detachment from the feelings of others.

blue

Blue can reveal religious feelings and is often seen in the auras of psychics and other medical practitioners.

Compassion, idealism, intellect, integrity, and truth are reflected by clear blue. Self-control and the ability to rationalize emotional processes are also indicated when this color is present. With darker shades of blue, beware jealousy and mistrust, while lighter blue may betray a sense of hopelessness.

indigo

This color is associated with a trustworthy person for whom integrity is paramount and whose word is his or her bond. A particularly strong presence of indigo in a person's aura tells of a wise and committed individual. This is a person who will never let you down.

violet

Purple indicates a deeply spiritual and committed individual. The more purple, the more religious the person is likely to be. These colors—rarely present in large quantities—reveal raised awareness and a highly developed consciousness.

Lilac and the lighter shades of violet may suggest an unrealistic attitude to everyday life and an idealistic approach to relationships.

gray

A conventional attitude and lack of imagination are revealed by a gray aura. Health-wise, this is not the most auspicious of colors as it suggests depleted energies and a poor immune system. When gray appears, especially veering toward the darker, charcoal shade, there could also be a marked tendency to depression.

black

Black signifies dark thoughts and sinister motives. Just as we say figuratively that an angry or depressed person has a black cloud over his or her head, so to have black in one's aura is not a good sign. When black combines with the other colors it turns them dull and murky, suggesting that destructive passions are at work or that energy blocks are undermining health. Brown, too, is inauspicious for similar reasons.

The chakras

The theory of energy channels that flow through the body and meet at centers known as "chakras" is fundamental to Eastern medicine and philosophy. The chakras are believed to be in a vertical column, from the base of the spine up to the top of the head. There are seven major chakras, each related to specific physical, mental, and spiritual functions, and regulating the energy which keeps mind, body, and spirit holistically tuned.

The balance of energy

In a healthy body, where the chakras are in balance, the energy will flow freely right around the system, through the chakras and along the meridians, or energy channels. However, physical problems, emotional traumas, and the stresses of everyday life can all undermine the body's delicate balance, and the chakras may become blocked, depleted, or overloaded. When this happens, physical or psychological ill health will follow.

When we are ill, the condition of our chakras enables us to trace the root of our malaise. Because each chakra is associated with a particular part of the anatomy, such as a gland or an organ in the body, any imbalances in the energy flow through the chakras will create a domino effect and manifest themselves as problems in their related areas. Aches and pains in a particular part of the body suggest that its corresponding chakra is in a state of imbalance. Conversely, if we can pinpoint which chakra is malfunctioning, we can deduce from that all the anatomical areas that are likely to be affected, either at present or in the future, unless matters are corrected.

In addition, all our emotions, creative impulses, spiritual feelings, and intuitive understanding correspond to the seven energy centers and will, therefore, be similarly affected by the condition of the chakras.

Color and the chakras

Each chakra is linked to a color whose vibrational frequency matches its own resonance. When a blockage or imbalance of energy occurs, the frequency of the affected chakra is thrown out of tempo. This can be restored by stimulating that chakra with its corresponding color through visualization, the use of crystals, or a healer.

Rather than waiting to use these techniques until we are physically or psychologically out of sorts, we can use color as a therapeutic tool to keep our chakras working efficiently and to develop their strength and power. When well-balanced and well-tuned, the chakras will ensure that our minds and bodies are in harmony. They will enhance our health, balance our emotions, boost our effectiveness, encourage inner growth, and heighten our perception and spiritual awareness. According to Eastern teaching, maintaining our chakras is the key to health, happiness, and well-being.

Wheels of power

Chakras are said to resemble disks that spin or pulsate as energy flows through them. The word itself is taken from Sanskrit and means "wheel."

The seven chakras and their correspondences

chakra	location	physiological association	hormonal stimulus	psychological response
base	base of spine	adrenals, rectum	adrenaline	fear or courage, self-awareness
sacral	lower abdomen	ovaries or testes, kidneys, bowel	sex hormones	pleasure, self-respect
solar plexus	solar plexus	pancreas, digestive tract	thymosin	compassion, self-love
heart	heart	thymus, immune system, circulation	insulin	happiness, self-worth
throat	throat	thyroid, respiratory system	thyroxine	inspiration, self-expression
brow	forehead	pituitary, eyes, sinuses	stimulating hormones	intuition, self-responsibility
crown	top of head	pineal gland, brain, nervous system	melatonin	enlightenment, self-knowledge

Activating the chakras

Color can be used to heal the whole system or to activate individual chakras. By stimulating a particular chakra, you can affect the organ, gland, or other part of the body associated with it. For example, someone suffering from a sore throat could boost their throat chakra with blue—its corresponding color. They might wear more blue clothing, visualize a ray of blue light focused on their neck, or hold a piece of lapis lazuli to their throat for several minutes each day. Other aspects of the chakra will also be strengthened by application of the relevant color. If blue is applied to the throat chakra, powers of communication and self-expression will become more effective, and creativity will flourish.

In cases where a chakra is overloaded, there will be an excess of energy from that center, resulting in some form of hyperactivity. Activating that chakra with its own color will only further exacerbate the condition, so what is required here is to tone down the chakra's resonance. This is achieved by retuning the chakra with its related complementary color.

The rainbow ladder

The seven chakras work in conjunction with each other. None can function in isolation, but together they form a complete and holistic system. They act somewhat like the rungs of a ladder—leading us to different levels of physical and mental development and well-being.

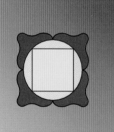

Base chakra

Located at the base of the spine, this energy center is also known as the root chakra because its action enables us to ground, or root, ourselves. The energy from this chakra works down the sexual organs, legs, and feet to connect us with the ground. Survival is the key instinct associated with the base chakra. When its energies are balanced, we feel settled, safe, and secure. Walking around barefoot will enhance our sense of connectedness, and stimulate this center.

	underactive	overactive
symptoms	*lack of energy* *lack of enthusiasm* *eating disorders*	*impatience* *aggression* *hyperactivity* *food intolerances*
color application	*use red*	*use green, then balance with a little red*

Sacral chakra

Sited in the pelvis, just below the navel, the sacral chakra is linked to the reproductive system and is associated with creativity and procreation. This center is also known as the spleen chakra and finds a correspondence in the muscles and organs that are involved in eliminating waste from the body.

Here is the seat of our pleasures and desires, of our sexual urges, feelings, and emotions. When this chakra is well balanced, we feel good about ourselves and are able to take pleasure from our relationships and dealings with others. Because elimination is the key to this energy center, learning to let go of our negative thoughts brings health and progress into our lives.

	underactive	overactive
symptoms	*introversion*	*arrogance*
	feelings of inadequacy	*pride*
	harboring grudges	*sexual dominance*
color application	*use orange*	*use blue, then balance with a little orange*

Solar plexus chakra

Lying just below the rib cage, this energy center is linked to the organs of the digestive system and aids the assimilation of nutrients in the body.

A healthy solar plexus chakra imbues us with vitality and ensures that we are confident and empowered with self-esteem. Personal warmth plus the ability to trust and to give out unconditional affection to others, are the results of balanced energies here. When out of balance, we can expect all manner of nutritional problems, ranging from anorexia through peptic ulcers to diabetes.

	underactive	overactive
symptoms	*loneliness*	*addiction*
	guilt	*hot temper*
	psychosomatic illnesses	*digestive problems*
color application	*use yellow*	*use violet, then balance with a little yellow*

Heart chakra

Residing at the level of the heart, the energies of this center play a pivotal role in the chakra system. Physically, the heart chakra influences the heart, the circulatory system in general, and the lungs. Esoterically, it integrates the life forces from the basal centers with those of the upper chakras by sifting and blending them together.

When this chakra's energies are out of balance, we experience bitterness and resentment toward others. Harmonious function, on the other hand, encourages us to love ourselves and to accept our faults for what they are. When these energies are in balance, we feel at peace with ourselves and with others.

	underactive	overactive
symptoms	*possessiveness*	*jealousy*
	anxiety	*anger*
	indifference	*circulatory problems*
color application	*use green*	*use green, then balance with a little pink*

Throat chakra

Located in the center of the neck, this chakra is associated with language, communication, and personal expression. Its energies influence the respiratory system, mouth, teeth, and ears.

Sore throats, bronchitis and hearing problems are often signs of a blocked chakra. When the energies here are out of balance, we find it difficult to get our point of view across. Writer's block, getting a lump in one's throat, or crying from anger or frustration are typical of imbalances here. When functioning correctly, this chakra will enable us to perceive the truth, will hone our powers of expression and encourage us to channel our inspired ideas into creative achievements.

	underactive	overactive
symptoms	*shyness*	*frustration*
	fear of change	*feeling of being trapped*
	moodiness	*fanaticism*
color application	*use blue*	*use orange then balance with a little blue*

Brow chakra

At the center of the forehead and between the eyebrows resides the brow chakra, which is also known as the third eye and, as such, deals with insight and objective awareness. Issues of sight and perception also come under the brow chakra's sphere of influence.

A blockage in this chakra will manifest in an inability to focus on the task in hand. A distorted viewpoint, visual defects, headaches and sinus problems are linked to the energies here being out of kilter. When well developed and working harmoniously, the brow chakra widens our perspective, brings us visionary talents and heightens our powers of intuition.

	underactive	overactive
symptoms	*envy* *absent-mindedness* *headaches*	*mental confusion* *bad dreams* *lack of concentration*
color application	*use indigo*	*use peach, then balance with a little indigo*

Crown chakra

Sited at the very top of the head, the crown chakra deals with our intellect and conscious awareness of life. Development of this chakra leads to a state of bliss known as Nirvana – perfect understanding and union with the cosmos. Though many strive to achieve this elevated stage of being, few succeed completely.

Problems associated with brain functioning, such as epilepsy or senile dementia, are thought to correspond to blockages in the energies of this chakra. A lack of interest, a negative attitude and a bleak outlook are also linked to imbalances here. Only those who reach Nirvana by activating their crown chakra can be said to be truly enlightened.

	underactive	overactive
symptoms	*negativity* *shame* *depression*	*over-developed imagination* *schizophrenia*
color application	*use violet*	*use yellow, then balance with a little violet*

Using the healing power of color

You can use the healing power of color at home. The simplest way is to wear the color in your clothes. Sitting under the light from a colored lightbulb can also be very effective. Or you could fix a filter or some colored cellophane of the required color over a lamp and shine it onto the affected area of your body. Make sure the cellophane does not touch the bulb, and keep the wattage low, or there could be a danger of setting it alight. If you are using a lamp in this way, limit your exposure to between five to ten minutes at at time. Too much exposure can be as detrimental as too little.

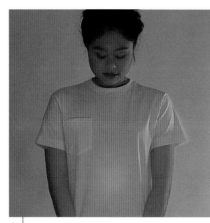

A short spell under a red light can invigorate jaded spirits, although too long could be detrimental to you.

Some people like to focus on a color card and others use visualizing techniques, holding the color in their heads and surrounding themselves in an imaginary cloud of blue or green, or whatever they feel their body needs at that time. Some healers are able to transmit color from their own bodies onto their patients, and many can even do this as absent healing, simply with the power of thought.

Whatever system you use, it is important to understand how our bodies are affected by different color energies. And remember, too, that colors can harm as well as heal.

Harmonizing the chakras

There are several ways you can apply color to heal your chakras. Most you can do for yourself at home. In some cases, though, you may wish to consult a professional therapist. First, decide which of the seven centers you feel need to be worked on and then try one the following suggestions:

○ *Wear clothes in the color of the affected chakra.*

○ *Lie down, and place seven felt squares in each of the colors of the rainbow on your body in line with the chakras. Relax, breathe deeply, and, with each breath, imagine you are taking colored rays from the felt into your body. (You may need to fold the indigo to fit over your forehead.)*

○ *Place crystals of corresponding colors directly over the affected energy center, again while you lie down and relax. (See pages 82–89 to find out more about healing with crystals.)*

○ *Massage with Aura-Soma Equilibrium oils in the colors required. (For futher information on Aura-Soma color therapy see pages 102–109.)*

○ *Stick a sheet of colored acetate (in the appropriate color) over a table lamp, as described above, and sit with the colored light shining on you for ten minutes each day.*

○ *Stand appropriate Color Insight Cards on your desk at work, and focus on them from time to time throughout the day.*

red

Red has a stimulating and vitalizing action and may be used to energize the body. It produces warmth, so is useful in the treatment of colds and chills. Anemia, bronchitis, ulcers, and constipation may all be treated with this color.

Use red to lift depression, lethargy, and tiredness, to boost the circulation, stimulate a sluggish digestion, and promote liver function. Red is also cheering; it excites the nervous system, gives

confidence, and increases feelings of optimism and well-being. Use it to stir the life force and the sex drive, but beware—too much red can overexcite the passions and lead to rage. It can also cause headaches and is inadvisable for use in cases of high blood pressure or in any condition where inflammation has occurred.

orange

Like red, orange is warming and energizing, but it is gentler and can be used in cases where red would be too harsh. This is an excellent color to apply to a sprained muscle, to relieve joint pains, and to energize the body

when cold. Orange is of benefit in arthritic or rheumatic conditions, and in cases where circulation is poor. It is also a great nerve tonic, good at combating mental sluggishness and nervous exhaustion while calming anxiety. Use orange to promote intestinal activity and to kick-start sluggish renal function. It can be of benefit in respiratory ailments, helping to clear the airways and alleviate bronchial or asthmatic problems.

Too much orange, however, can overstimulate the mucous linings and have an adverse effect on the thyroid gland.

yellow

Yellow is a general blood tonic, useful for intestinal or gastric conditions, for activating the digestive system, and for helping to reduce bloating after a meal. Because this color is associated with the mental processes, it can pep up those suffering from nervous exhaustion. As a color from the warm end of the spectrum, yellow can also help to raise energy levels and boost self-esteem. In addition, it re-balances the nervous system.

Too much yellow, though, can overstimulate, so it is best avoided when feverish or where heart problems are suspected. It

is also aging for the skin and may cause dizziness. Too little yellow can lead to water-retention, depression, and forgetfulness and is also associated with an underactive thyroid system.

green

With its calming and soothing effect, green is the ultimate blood-cooler. In healing, this color has many uses. Its balancing properties realign the body's energies, relieving exhaustion yet aiding relaxation. Green has a beneficial action on the kidneys and is helpful in renal problems. Use it to ease headaches, to control nervous tension, and to promote sleep. Wrapping a green blanket around a sick child or teaching her to "think of green" can help

to soothe a high temperature and will encourage the healing process to take place.

People who are in any way depressed should not be exposed to too much of this color. An excess of green may cause a tendency to arthritis. Too little green, though, can bring on anxiety and may even hasten thinning of the bones.

blue

Blue has antiseptic powers. It purifies the blood and may be used on cuts and grazes to cleanse wounds. It is a general cleanser and protector, and very useful against viral or bacteriological infections. This

color is particularly beneficial around the neck, to ease a sore throat. Use it to calm over-excitement and hyperactivity, to soothe a headache, or to bring down a high temperature.

Because it has a cooling and "lowering" action, blue is best avoided by those whose blood pressure is low or who are suffering from colds or chills. Too much blue can depress the spirits, and while a lack of blue is associated with bronchial disorders, too much is linked with asthmatic conditions. The deeper the blue, the more efficacious it is against stomach disorders, feverish conditions, and muscle fatigue.

indigo

Indigo continues the action of blue, as it, too, is cooling and astringent, but its effects go further because this color has a sedative, almost narcotic, effect. This is why indigo and blue are so useful in treating insomnia. Use indigo to calm the nerves, to control anger and aggression, and to help lower high blood pressure. In addition, indigo helps strengthen the lymph system and can be effective in clearing the sinuses.

Conditions of the eye, such as cataracts, and of the ear, nose, and throat respond well to this color. Too much indigo, however, can lower the spirits, and it is therefore not recommended for cases of depression.

violet

Like green and blue, violet also has a cleansing and antiseptic action. It helps to purify the blood and even—it is claimed— has the power to arrest the development of tumors. Moreover, it stimulates bone growth and encourages damaged tissue to rebuild itself.

Violet relieves congestion, helps reduce headaches brought on by nervous strain, and is beneficial in lessening nervous excitability. Those who are highly strung benefit from

violet's soothing effects. In addition, violet can be used to combat ailments of the bladder, ease skin problems, and relieve sciatic pain. Lighter shades are particularly useful in cases of shock where the body needs to be warmed and stimulated. A lack of this color is associated with anger and irritability, while too much can overstimulate the imagination.

white

When in doubt as to which color to use, think of white—the general energizer. White may be used safely as a cleansing, purifying, and strengthening agent, and because it embodies all the colors of the spectrum, it will also act as a protector while boosting the overall energies of the body.

If you are low in energy, cold, tired, or depressed, wrap a red scarf around your shoulders to give an instant boost.

Using the healing power of color

Healing with crystals and gemstones

Regarded by the ancients as "frozen light," crystals are solid color energies. As storehouses of power, able to both absorb and release energy, they have been used in healing throughout history.

It is believed that the electromagnetic pulse given off by a gem enables it, when placed on or near the skin, to affect the electrical resonance of the internal organs of the body. By matching an organ's vibrations, a crystal can fine-tune it and readjust its frequency, boosting weakened action or calming overactivity. In this way, crystals and gemstones help to correct the energy flows in our bodies and can play a valuable role in rebalancing both the aura and the chakras.

Traditionally, the curative powers of gemstones were matched by their color to particular diseases or to the specific anatomical areas they were designed to cure. Red stones like garnet and ruby, were therefore linked to the blood and used to treat hemorrhages and ailments of the heart and circulatory system. Jaundice, a symptom of liver dysfunction, which causes a yellow discoloring of the skin, was treated with the yellow–brown stone topaz.

We can use this same principle of "like cures like" to match the color of a crystal to its corresponding chakra. The green stones of emerald and jade, for example, will work with the heart chakra, while the blue of turquoise has a greater affinity with the throat chakra.

The healing properties of crystals

The uses to which we can put crystals are many, but in terms of healing, it is generally recognized that gems have the ability to help

- *balance the aura and the energy centers of the chakras*
- *remove blockages of the mind, body, and spirit*
- *calm our emotions*
- *channel our thoughts and feelings*
- *stimulate mental processes*
- *give out healing power*
- *spark energy*
- *bring us courage and strength*
- *induce sweet dreams*
- *facilitate visualization and encourage meditation*

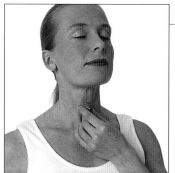

Linked to the throat chakra, turquoise aids speech and clarity of expression. It is generally associated with communication.

Worn as a pendant, jade resonates with the heart chakra. It fosters serenity and encourages true love.

Using crystals

Use gemstones in the following healing ways:

° Hold the crystals in your hands and absorb their gentle, restorative energies. You can stroke them, caress them, and use them as worry beads, and feel your stress being drawn out through your fingertips.

° Wear crystals as jewelry in their own right, or pop them in a pocket, where they will go on working quietly and unobtrusively.

° Place your crystals on a desk or a shelf to admire them. Just looking at their dazzling beauty can be enough to raise the spirits. Moonstones, agates, or amethysts placed by the bed are useful aids to peaceful sleeping and are conducive to dreaming, as their action calms anxieties and soothes excitability.

° Hold or place crystals on your skin (see below and left), either to help ease localized pain or match to stones to their appropriate chakra sites.

Buying crystals

Because crystals resonate on individual frequencies, buying a gemstone is a highly personal affair. If you find yourself drawn to one particular crystal more than any other in the store, it is probably because you are in tune with it. This means its unique resonance matches your own vibrations, and so it will work with you that much more effectively. So, however much or little you are spending on a gemstone, always follow your instincts. No matter how big or how small it may be, always go for the crystal that sings its song especially for you.

Amethyst has many therapeutic qualities, but its rich, violet color gives it a natural affinity with the brow chakra.

How different crystals heal

Although every single crystal is unique, each family of gemstones shares a similar quality of energy and exerts a similar type of effect. It is said that there is a crystal for every situation, and, interestingly, we tend to be instinctively drawn to the stone we need, whether we are stressed, run down, or just requiring a bit of an emotional boost. Ancient wisdom has taught us that crystals have specific actions and that some are more suited to particular problems than others.

Rose quartz, for example, can help to soothe a headache; red jasper has a grounding action; and lapis lazuli counteracts negative emotions. When we understand the active, healing properties of crystals, we can harness their energies and bring harmony into our lives.

Crystal cleansing

Crystals need periodic cleansing to remove any negative energies they may have absorbed from their surroundings and from other people. For a start, they must be cleansed when they are first purchased in order to disperse any negative energy already collected, and then again periodically, according to how much and how often they are used in healing. If they are not cleaned regularly, they will visibly lose their luster and become "clogged up" and ineffective. If you wear your crystal, you may need to cleanse it at least once a week and even more frequently if you are going through physical or emotional problems. Crystals that are on display, however, may not require such assiduous

agate

grounding ∘ energy ∘ base chakra

This stone encourages us to raise our awareness and open up to new ideas. The agate inspires us to find new ways of looking at the world and so is of immense value to anyone working in the creative field; writers, designers, and artists alike. Moreover, the agate promotes vitality and helps us to boost our energy levels, giving it a special affinity with the base chakra. Use it to "ground" yourself when you are looking for a sense of permanence and stability, or simply when you need to get a grip on reality. Wear it close to your skin when you feel that either your physical or emotional security is in need of shoring up. Hold it in your hand for ten minutes each day to help balance your energy centers and to bring a calming influence to your body and soul.

Alternative crystals: hematite, garnet, bloodstone, ruby

attention. Cleaning them once a month to restore their potency and luster may be enough.

There are several ways to cleanse a crystal, and the salesperson will be able to advise you. One method is to hold the stone under clear running water for about three minutes. Alternatively, some may be soaked in salt water overnight. Leaving a gemstone in the garden in the moonlight, or on a windowsill to catch the rays of the sun, will recharge the crystal.

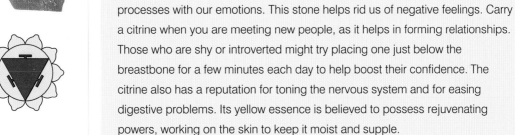

topaz

courage ○ virility ○ sacral chakra

Topaz brings out our loving and affectionate instincts and is claimed to boost virility and sex appeal. The ancients saw the topaz as a symbol of honesty and fidelity and used it for healing stomach or intestinal problems. It is considered to give out a tranquilizing effect and believed to be of help in easing catarrhal problems, asthma, and nervous tension. As its golden orange tones link it to the sacral chakra, this stone may be used to combat fear. Wear it as a ring or keep a small piece in a pocket and hold it in your hand whenever you need courage.

Alternative crystals: tiger's eye, carnelian

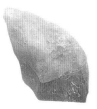

citrine

confidence ○ digestion ○ solar plexus chakra

The yellow energies of the citrine act as a fulcrum and balance our intellectual processes with our emotions. This stone helps rid us of negative feelings. Carry a citrine when you are meeting new people, as it helps in forming relationships. Those who are shy or introverted might try placing one just below the breastbone for a few minutes each day to help boost their confidence. The citrine also has a reputation for toning the nervous system and for easing digestive problems. Its yellow essence is believed to possess rejuvenating powers, working on the skin to keep it moist and supple.

Alternative crystals: aventurine, smoky quartz

jade

love ∘ circulation ∘ heart chakra

Jade's therapeutic action promotes our sense of caring for others and encourages feelings of unconditional love. On a physical level, green jade is believed to strengthen the functions of the heart and the kidneys and generally tone the circulatory system. Indeed, it has a reputation as a blood tonic and purifier and regulates blood pressure by reducing hypertension. Keep a piece of jade by your bedside to bolster your immune system. Hold it against your skin to balance your emotions and bring you serenity and peace of mind. Or wear it as the ancient wise men did, to attract loyalty and support.

Alternative crystals: malachite, rose quartz, emerald

turquoise

communication ∘ protection ∘ throat chakra

Turquoise is prized for its holistic qualities and its powers of protection. Though our forefathers wore it as a safeguard against what they perceived to be evil entities, in modern-day terms we see the protective powers of this stone as lying in its ability to absorb radiation and other atmospheric pollution of our time. In healing, turquoise is a great strengthener of the whole system. It possesses a pick-me-up effect and is even said to have the ability to kick-start tissue regeneration. Its blue coloring links it with the throat chakra, which makes it an invaluable stimulus for communication. Hold a piece at your throat for a few minutes each day to encourage clarity of expression. Carry a piece if you have to attend an audition or are giving a talk. Turquoise is a useful aid for writers, singers, actors, and all those who make their living by the power of the word.

Alternative crystals: lapis lazuli, celestite, aquamarine, sapphire

amethyst

intuition ∘ relaxation ∘ brow chakra

It is little wonder that this gemstone has been held in high esteem throughout the ages, for the virtues of the amethyst are many, and its benefits are of inestimable value to mind, body and spirit. Amethyst has a calming effect, helping to cool tempers and control high emotions. It is a wonderful aid to restful sleep; a piece kept on the bedside table or, even better, under the pillow, is a must for those who suffer from sleepless nights. With its rich purple coloring, amethyst can be used to heighten intuition. Hold a piece to your forehead, at the center of your brow, to give you a more balanced outlook and to activate your third eye. Used in this way when meditating, amethyst will help your visualizations become sharp and focused. Also wear the stone to ease sinusitis and the congestion of a head cold. A piece by the computer is believed to absorb emissions of radiation.

Alternative crystals: azurite

diamond

enlightenment ∘ harmony ∘ crown chakra

It is no coincidence that diamonds are frequently worn in tiaras and regal crowns, for this dazzling gem is linked to the crown chakra. As the diamond scintillates and catches the light, so it conjures the quintessential enlightenment that we strive toward in developing and energizing our seventh chakra. The diamond is the stone of wisdom and has enjoyed a reputation of purity and perfection. It was said by the ancients to bring strength and courage and to further hope and reconciliation. As a promoter of honesty and loyalty, it is with good reason that the diamond is the most popular stone for engagement rings.

Not as costly as the diamond, but perhaps more efficacious, is clear quartz (see pages 88–89). This humble stone is able not only to resonate with the crown chakra but also to retune and harmonize the entire system.

Alternative crystals: clear quartz

Quartz: the master crystal

Quartz has been used for thousands of years as a channeling tool

Packed with powerful energies, clear quartz has been used for thousands of years as a channeling tool. Quartz is a master stone and undisputably a most useful crystal to have around. If you can afford only one stone, then choose a clear quartz, preferably a long crystal, about 3 in. (7 cm) long, and with a clear, pointed end.

Clearing energy blockages

Quartz crystal is an especially beneficial all-round stone for stimulating the chakras and clearing blocked energy points. Once you have matched the problem to the relevant chakra, hold the pointed end of the quartz against that part of your body and visualize the blockage dissolving and clearing away. Now channel white light and fresh energy through the crystal and into the body. See the energy flowing freely and guide it through by slowly moving the piece of quartz upward to balance each of the other chakras in turn.

You may repeat this exercise as often as you need to. You may like to try playing some soothing, inspirational music quietly in the background to help induce the right mood. Burning your favorite incense or aromatherapy oils, too, will encourage relaxation and strengthen your powers of visualization at the same time. One final reminder: do wash your crystals before and after this exercise. They will be working very hard for you and will need to be at their most potent for your exercise. Then they will need to be cleansed once again when you have finished.

Quartz is an invaluable tool in meditation. Focus on it to help open your mind and release your creative imagination and potential.

Some uses of quartz crystal:

- *as a channeling tool*
- *to magnify psychic energy*
- *to help draw out pain*
- *to heal emotional wounds*
- *to put right physical imbalances*
- *to aid the memory*
- *to protect, inspire, or boost communication*
- *to stimulate the chakras*

Crystal balancing exercise

If you have two pieces of quartz, you can use them to help tone and realign your whole system.

1. Find a comfortable spot to lie down, and spread out a blanket or towel. Place the first piece of quartz just above where your head will be, its pointed end directed toward your head. Place the other piece a little distance away from where your feet will be, with the pointed end toward your body. Lie down comfortably, full-length, between the two crystals, heels together and arms at your side, with hands palm-side up. Push the small of your back down toward the floor.

2. Visualize energy in the form of white light being drawn up from the crystal at your feet, through your soles and into your body. Feel the energy warming your body as it passes up through your legs to your abdomen. Imagine it pushing its way through your muscles and veins and each of your chakras in turn, clearing any blockages along its route. Slowly draw the energy up through your body to your head and out through the second crystal above your head. Pause and breathe deeply, feeling your system clear and all your channels free and unblocked. Take your time, there is no need to rush.

3. Repeat the process, but this time draw the energy down from the top crystal in through your head and into your body. As you breathe, imagine the white light streaming through your body and out to your aura. Visualize the rainbow of colors around your body being brightened and enhanced by new energy giving your aura vibrant new life. Work the energy down through your body, around your aura, and out through your toes to be received by the crystal at your feet.

4. Breathe rhythmically, and close down your chakras one at a time from the crown to the base. If you feel you want to drift off, then do so. If you feel energized and you want to stretch, do that. Spend the next five minutes or so doing whatever your body needs, and then slowly get up. Keep movements slow and gentle. Once on your feet again, take a deep breath, hold for a count of seven, and then slowly release it. As you do so, visualize your aura expanding around you in fine tendrils of luminous color. Finally, raise your arms high over your head and slowly lower them to inscribe a circle of light and protection around your body.

Creative visualization

Creative visualization can restore body and mind to a state of balance

Using nothing more than the power of our thoughts, we can experience sensations and recreate situations in our mind's eye that can actually trigger physical reactions in our hormonal systems and body chemistry. This technique is known as creative visualization and is used extensively in alternative healing to improve health and well-being.

Researchers have shown that, through creative visualization, we can lower high blood pressure, ease stress, change our moods, sharpen awareness, and restore the body and mind to a state of balance. Healers who work with color therapy use creative visualization to transmit energy to their clients. They intuitively sense where the client's energy-flows are low or blocked and, with the power of thought, are able to release a stream of light, heat or color which helps the individual's healing processes to take place.

You do not have to be a healer to take advantage of this method of healing, for we all have the ability to use creative visualization on a daily basis. All it takes is a little practice. Try the following color visualization exercises, which have been devised to build your confidence, lift your moods, and revitalize your energies.

red	orange	yellow	green

- *social, physical, or sexual energy*
- *stamina*
- *willpower*
- *strength*
- *vitality*

- *social interaction*
- *friendliness*
- *happiness*
- *adaptability*
- *attractiveness*

- *intellect*
- *mental stimulation*
- *objectivity*
- *concentration*

- *calmness*
- *growth*
- *success*
- *balance*
- *unconditional love*

blue	indigo	violet

- *communication*
- *peace*
- *relaxation*
- *wisdom*
- *protection*

- *inspiration*
- *new ideas*
- *understanding*
- *spiritual balance*

- *dignity*
- *self-respect*
- *enlightenment*
- *psychic awareness*
- *good luck*

Task accentuation

You can use visualization techniques to improve your performance of a task, whether work-related or personal. If special effort is required, this exercise will help you go the extra mile.

1. Identify the type of task you are about to undertake and identify its associated color. For example, writing a letter is a form of communication, which is associated with the throat chakra and the color blue.

2. Sit or lie quietly and take a few slow, deep breaths. Feel your shoulders drop and your muscles relax as the tension eases out of your body.

3. Imagine the color in your mind. Focus on that color; make it stronger and more vibrant. Make the color increase in size and feel yourself being drawn toward it. You may want to float, walk, or dive into the color. Go with what your mind wants to do and simply

immerse yourself into its pool of light. Feel it wash all over you, flowing through your body, fusing with you until you become the color itself.

4. Step out of the color, and, as you walk away, imagine that you are going about your task. Recreate the steps involved, the words, actions, and feelings required to carry out the job, and let inspiration guide you through. Visualize the color all around you as you go about your task. Now see yourself having accomplished the work successfully. You're feeling satisfied, glowing with a great sense of achievement and you know the task has been a terrific success.

5. Take a slow deep breath, open your eyes, and begin the task for real. Follow the steps you imagined, and bring the color back into your mind now and again as a prompt while you work.

Standing your ground

H ere is an exercise for those times when you require courage. Perhaps you have to give a speech to a committee, or you need to ask your boss for a raise, stand up to a bully, or generally assert yourself. Whatever the situation, this exercise can help to boost your confidence and give you the necessary *gravitas* that will make people hold you in higher regard. This is an exercise you can do quickly and efficiently at any time, in any place, without anyone even noticing. What *you* will notice, however, is that as a consequence others will treat you with respect. Try it five or ten minutes before you are required to stand your ground.

1. *Sit or stand with both feet flat on the floor so that you feel thoroughly grounded and connected with the earth.*

Take a long, slow breath through your nose. As you inhale, imagine that you are breathing in all the colors of the rainbow. See the colors entering your body one by one with the air in your breath as you inhale. Imagine that the colors are strong and vibrant—now make them even more vivid, each molecule pulsating with life.

2. *Push this breath down, past your diaphragm and into your stomach.*

Push the air in your lungs downward so that you feel your stomach extending outward, and hold it there for a slow count of five. Now open your mouth slightly and start to exhale, slowly and steadily. Bring the breath up to the heart chakra, focus on it there, and push all that radiant light back out through your body. Feel the colored rays streaming out

With practice you will be able to flash this protective ring into place in an instant whenever you need its protection. With your rainbow around you, you will feel taller and more powerful, but at the same time also more graceful, able to put your point of view across with confidence and consideration.

all around you, enclosing you in a rainbow cocoon of light. Hold on to the feeling of being surrounded in all the colors of the spectrum.

3. Take another breath and repeat the process.

With every successive breath you take, push the boundary of your color cocoon farther out than before, until you can sense that you are enveloped in a rainbow bubble that extends far beyond your physical body. Hold that cocoon around you for as long as you feel you need to, in order to gain the courage and confidence to perform the task or chore ahead of you.

If you feel the effect fading during the day, you can also, if you like, boost its intensity every now and again simply by imagining you are turning up the dimmer switch of a light.

Closing chakras

When the task for which you have prepared is over, you should check your heart chakra and make sure it has closed.

Chakras open as we "give out" or "receive" energy and we must remember to close them again afterward to conserve our strength.

Imagine that this chakra is a flower in full bloom. Gently allow it to close its petals one by one.

You can do this with each chakra, starting from the base and working up to the crown. In fact, this is a very good exercise to carry out as part of an ongoing routine maintenance program for both your aura and chakra systems.

Call to the Sun

Harness the energy of light to revitalize your body and mind

Call to the Sun is an exercise drawing on the power of light—the source of all colors. Although it is best carried out on a sunny morning, the benefits of this technique can be felt at any time, as it will help you to center yourself and revitalize your body and your mind. To perform it you need light, preferably light from the sun. But remember, never look directly into the sun, as that can damage your eyes. Performing this exercise outside in the open air is ideal, but standing by a window can be effective, too. If the sun is behind a cloud, face in its direction if you can. On a really gray day, a lamp may be used to substitute for the sun. This is particularly beneficial to those who suffer from SAD (seasonal affective disorder), who should try to practice this simple exercise on a daily basis.

1

This exercise is especially useful for:

- blowing away winter blues
- boosting physical vitality
- harnessing mental power and energy
- finding hope, direction, inspiration, or peace of mind
- promoting a sense of well-being

Draw on the Sun's power

1. Face the sun with your feet slightly apart, arms at your sides. Shut your eyes and raise your head to feel the revitalizing rays gently bathing your face.

2. Begin the rhythmic breathing exercise. Breathe in slowly through your nose, hold the breath for a count of three, and then breathe out slowly through your mouth. Pause. Repeat three times. Drop your head and bring your hands together in front of you.

3. Taking a slow breath in, raise your head and arms out and upward, drawing a circle around yourself. With your head raised and your hands meeting high above your head, hold your breath for a count of three.

4. Slowly release your breath as you drop your arms to meet in front, and lower your head to rest your chin on your chest. Repeat steps 3 and 4 three times.

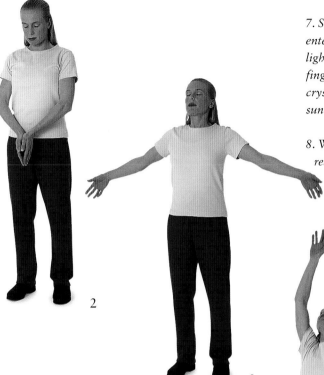

2

3

7. Spread your arms out, feel the warming rays entering through the palms of your hands. Play the light through your fingers. Smile as you wiggle your fingers and imagine running your hands through a crystal stream. Breathe rhythmically as you draw the sun into your body and feel linked into the cosmos.

8. Were you jaded or tired? Have you lost direction, reached a crossroad, or need an answer to a question? Are you afraid, in need of courage or inspiration? Whatever you are seeking, hold it in your mind now and ask to find a solution. Play the light through your fingers and feel the energy radiating around you.

9. Drop your hands to your side; repeat the rhythmic breathing three times. Finally, raise your arms and stretch.

7

8

5. Relax and breathe normally. With your eyes still shut and head toward the sun, feel the rays of light entering through your face, down into your chest, through your thorax and into your legs. Now, bring that warm energy back up through your legs; feel it rise up your spine. Hold that energy in your chest; feel it warming and spreading through your body.

6. Visualize the circle you have drawn around yourself with your arms. Allow the rays to emanate out from your center and to flow and fill that circle around you. Imagine that halo of golden energy all around your body. Feel yourself being energized, empowered, and enriched by the golden light. Feel yourself drawn to the sun, fusing into the universe.

Dreaming in color

Dreams connect us to our collective subconscious

Theories abound as to why we dream. Some people think dreams function as a safety valve, helping us to release the tensions of the day. Others say that dreaming is a kind of elaborate filing system, storing away important experiences and discarding those that are irrelevant to our needs. Still others believe that our dreams are like video recordings, allowing us, in the quiet moments of our sleep, to make sense of the events that have taken place in our busy, waking lives.

Link to the subconscious

Perhaps the most enduring belief about dreaming is that it puts us in touch with the workings of our subconscious minds, or, as Carl Jung described it, links us with the collective unconscious, giving us access to information that would not ordinarily be available to us on a conscious level. But, despite the theories, no one really knows why we dream at all.

There is, however, a lot that we do know about dreams and dreaming. For example, researchers can tell us how long a dream lasts. They can show precisely when in the sleep process a dream begins and ends. They have discovered the most common themes people dream about. And they can even tell us who is likely to dream about what.

There are other factors we know about dreaming: that if we are deprived of dream-sleep, we become irritable, lose concentration, and grow ill. We know, too, that our dreams are delivered to us in a strange and wonderful language, not of words, but of imagery and pictorial significance.

What our dreams mean

In our dreams, each picture is a symbol, a concentrated message compressed into an image. Every picture can tell a whole story. To dream of a house, for instance, is symbolic of dreaming about our own body, its condition reflecting our own health and state of mind. The attic represents the head, clutter and cobwebs suggesting a need for a fresh intellectual stimulus. Equally, the kitchen is said to represent our feelings of well-being; the bedroom, perhaps, refers to our sex life; and an unlit cellar those dark, hidden instincts or talents that have yet to see the light of day. Among all these images, color has its own role to play, for each color carries with it information that will add to, or help to explain, the message of the dream.

Dreaming in red

To see, for example, a red throw over a bed could be speaking a thousand silent words about the dreamer's feelings. Because red is the sign of passion, this image might be making a statement about the dreamer's emotional life or may imply a degree of eroticism, sexual need, or even of anger toward a partner. But red is also the sign of danger, so this image could be warning the dreamer that feelings have reached fever pitch and that it is time to draw back emotionally. What happens in the rest of the dream would make it clear which of these aspects apply.

Dreaming in blue

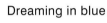

Blue is cooling, relaxing, and refreshing. To dream of this color may be suggesting that the body needs a rest. Perhaps if the dreamer has been excessively busy of late, his or her subconscious may be warning that a vacation is required. Blue is also a sign of ambition: to fly in an azure blue sky is taken as a dream of achievement, where the dreamer acknowledges the successes in his or her life.

Dreaming in green

Green, perhaps in the form of a patch of grass or a flash of an emerald ring, might be a dream of hope, new growth, or fresh developments about to take place in one's waking life. However, green is also the color of envy, so the dream may be cautioning you about a jealous situation.

Dreaming in other colors

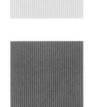

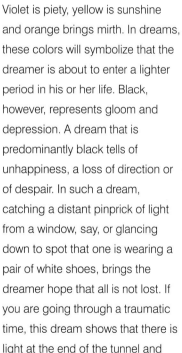

Violet is piety, yellow is sunshine and orange brings mirth. In dreams, these colors will symbolize that the dreamer is about to enter a lighter period in his or her life. Black, however, represents gloom and depression. A dream that is predominantly black tells of unhappiness, a loss of direction or of despair. In such a dream, catching a distant pinprick of light from a window, say, or glancing down to spot that one is wearing a pair of white shoes, brings the dreamer hope that all is not lost. If you are going through a traumatic time, this dream shows that there is light at the end of the tunnel and brings comfort and reassurance that matters will resolve themselves in time.

Just as in our waking lives, so in our dreams, too, colors carry their symbolic messages, and it pays us all to take note.

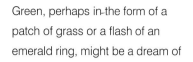
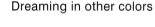

Therapy in Nature

From the delicate greenish white of the snowdrop in early spring to the flaming reds of autumn leaves, Nature is rich in ever-changing shades and tones. Flowers of every hue stand out against a backdrop of green—the color that is synonymous with Nature itself, soothing and calming with its tranquilizing effects.

Green, the universal balancer, is restful to the eye and promotes healing. Every garden, however small, has enormous therapeutic potential. Walking on a lawn or among trees in leaf enables us to recharge our nervous systems and restore harmony to body and mind.

It is from the light of the sun, Earth's great life-giver, that plants take energy which they put into growth and into the pigment of their blossom. As we gaze upon the petals of a flower, we absorb those energies and take in the healing properties of their colors. Just as we might use crystals or

Use color in the garden as you would when decorating a room—add reds for drama, blues for elegance, or pink and white accents to create a haven of serenity.

colored rays from a lamp to rebalance our systems, so the color of a flower can offer us healing energy.

Though perhaps we can never hope to reproduce the myriad tints of the natural world, we can capture some of its magic in our own gardens. And whether we choose a scheme that is monochromatic, themed into specific combinations, or massed with a variety of shape and bloom, we cannot fail to gain physical and spiritual benefits from bringing beauty and color into our lives.

Individual needs

What do you require from your garden—peace and tranquility or energy and invigoration? Careful planting, a little knowledge about flowers, and an awareness of the physical and psychological effects of color will help you achieve the required effect.

Remember that, like the colors at the warm end of the spectrum, flowers that are red, orange and yellow will excite and quicken your pulse. Since they are advancing colors they will also make your garden look smaller.

If you want a more calming setting or would like to give an illusion of space, choose colors from the cool end of the spectrum. Blues and violets, lifted with white, will give you space and create an atmosphere of elegance and serenity.

Changing light

The quality or intensity of sunlight from dawn to dusk can alter the appearance of the color of a flower through the day. A delphinium may appear sapphire blue at first light, cobalt in the midday sun, and ultraviolet just before nightfall. Changing weather conditions, as well as the differing light levels from one season to the next, have an impact on how we perceive the colors of Nature.

Plant and color combinations

For vibrance and drama

- red poppy
- rosa moyesii
- peony
- crocosmia
- geums
- hemerocallis
- tropaeolum
- salvia
- chaenomeles
- astilbe
- potentilla

For peace and tranquility

- plumbago
- solanum
- delphinium
- campanula
- petunia
- rosa iceberg
- anemone
- agapanthus
- datura
- buddleia
- ceanothus

For softness and romance

- jasmine
- lilac
- malva
- pink rose
- lavender
- lily
- camellia
- hydrangea
- wisteria
- clematis
- viola

For relaxation and informality

- artemesia
- hops
- cineraria
- aralia
- hypericum
- alchemilla
- hosta
- laburnum
- santolina
- ivy
- daffodil

Making a meal of color

One of the most natural ways of absorbing color is through the foods we eat. When we take in food, we are taking in energy, and some of that energy comes from the color of the food itself. So, when we need color healing, we should eat colors as part of our therapy. For example, if we feel tired and listless, eating red-colored foods will give us extra vitality. Equally, we can avoid foodstuffs containing the colors we know will worsen an existing condition. Red, we know, can cause headaches so, according to the theory, an individual who suffers with migraines might be wise to avoid eating red foods.

A healthy, balanced diet consists of eating a variety of foods. Balancing our system means ensuring that we eat as many different-colored foods as we can on a daily basis. "Eat five fruits or vegetables a day" is the health slogan of our times—simple advice to follow if we think of it as eating a rainbow a day.

Color and diet

There is a theory among certain color therapists that obesity is linked to an imbalance of color in the aura. People who are overweight, it is suggested, may have absorbed too much blue into their bodies and not enough red. If this theory is correct, increasing intake of healthy red foods, absorbing red light (see page 78), and drinking red solarized water may all be beneficial in helping to rebalance the aura.

Rainbow foods

Mixed salads, whether of fruits or vegetables, are more likely to keep the doctor at bay than the single proverbial apple. Moreover, a salad will also enable us to prepare a dish of many colors. When assembling the ingredients, though, it will soon become apparent that, while Nature yields an abundance of red, orange, yellow, and green produce, blue foods are quite rare.

As savoury blue vegetables are difficult to come by, add a few black grapes or black olives for indigo energy, or a handful of borage flowers for blue energy to complete the balance of colors on your plate. These flowers are edible and would not only complete the spectrum but also garnish the dish with their intense color and lovely, starry shapes. Blue fruits are more common, and putting together a rainbow dessert takes little effort. Some suggestions for each color are listed on the right. Blue, indigo, and violet are listed grouped together due to their comparative scarcity.

Solarized water

Another way of absorbing the properties of a color is to drink it. Color healers put great store in solarized water. Essentially, this is water charged with a color. It is done as follows:

1   *Decide what color your system needs and fill a glass of that color with water. If you cannot find a glass of your required color, you can use a filter—a sheet of colored cellophane attached around the outside of the glass will work just as well.*

2   *Place the glass on a sunny windowsill for at least two hours. Cover the top of the glass to prevent insects or dust falling into the water. During the winter or cooler weather, the glass may have to stand for several hours—perhaps even a whole day—to get enough sunlight to charge the water.*

3   *Solarize any color you need to give your body the color boost it requires. To ensure a constant supply, have a large container, or several glasses charging at the same time.*

red	orange	blue, indigo and violet	green	yellow
◦ cherries	◦ papaya	◦ eggplants	◦ apple	◦ lemon
◦ radish	◦ tangerine	◦ blueberries	◦ cucumber	◦ grapefruit
◦ red onion	◦ pumpkin	◦ currants	◦ cabbage	◦ mango
◦ red beans	◦ oranges	◦ beets	◦ spinach	◦ corn
◦ chilies	◦ nectarines	◦ olives	◦ olive	◦ banana
◦ tomatoes	◦ apricot	◦ plums	◦ lettuce	◦ cheese
◦ strawberries	◦ carrots		◦ grapes	◦ bread

The inspirational energies of Aura-Soma

If you have never associated physical well-being with sensual delight, then it is time to discover the uplifting effects of the Aura-Soma range. Aura-Soma is a holistic tool that works on many levels. It consists of a range of oils combining herbs, essences, and crystal energies in solutions of mesmerizing colors. As your poster shows, there are over ninety bottles in the Aura-Soma set. Each one is made up of two different colored substances, one resting above the other, so that the bottle appears to be divided in two. They are called Equilibrium bottles, not simply because their contents are held in balance with each other, but also because the stimulating properties of the oils help to harmonize the energies of the chakras and thus restore equanimity and balance to the body, mind, and soul.

It is the stunning rainbow of colors in all their different combinations that makes these oils immediately compelling and uplifting. To see them arranged on their glass shelves, lit up from behind like a stained-glass window, brings alive their gem like qualities. Simply looking at the bottles has a magical effects as their scintillating colors work their powers on you. But there is a great deal more to these Equilibrium bottles than just beauty alone.

Aura-Soma Equilibrium oils are linked to the chakras, and each is gently massaged into its corresponding area of the body.

Using Aura-Soma

Each Aura-Soma Equilibrium bottle contains a formula of powerful energies that promote well-being. This consists of essential oils infused with active plant and flower ingredients, as well as a fragrance, a crystal essence and two colors, one above the other.

Although it is recommended that you consult a qualified Aura-Soma practitioner in order to select bottles, your poster will give you some idea of their beauty and scope. Contact details for practitioners are listed at the end of this book.

Energy vibrations

The bottles are each linked to, and work on, the energy frequencies of one or more of the chakras. Their action is spiritually and emotionally restorative,

---

Caution

Although non-toxic, these oils are not for internal consumption and are intended for external application only. They may be used in conjunction with conventional medicine, but not as a substitute for treatment prescribed by your medical practitioner.

helping to rebalance the chakra centers and the auric field. Pages 104–109 contain a guide to each bottle shown on the poster, describing which chakra points and conditions it is suitable for.

Diagnostic properties

These bottles have another important function beyond imparting a sense of well-being, for they can act as development tools in their own right. Curiously enough, we are drawn intuitively to the bottles whose color energies resonate with our own psyche, our spiritual, emotional, and psychological needs. By selecting the bottle colors that attract us most, we are identifying, on a subconscious level, the very conditions we need to address to become fulfilled in our own lives. For example, choosing bottle 49, turquoise over violet, suggests that unresolved issues stand in the way of forming viable, loving relationships.

From out of the darkness

Aura-Soma was created by Vicky Wall, a seventh child of a seventh child. Vicky trained in both pharmacy and chiropody. She described how the concept came to her in 1983, while she was meditating. "Divide the waters," were the words that kept repeating themselves inside her head. Although she had no idea what this could mean, she later found herself in her laboratory, mixing oils and colors and herbal essences into little glass containers. The results were the first dazzlingly beautiful Equilibrium bottles. What is so truly remarkable about this fascinating event is that Vicky Wall was blind.

What does your choice mean?

The Aura-Soma Equilibrium bottles work on yet another level. They can take us on a spiritual journey. They can show us what our mission in life is, what lessons we need to learn, and what obstacles we must overcome in order to become whole and balanced people.

Select four bottles. Choose each one in turn, going for the one that calls to you or moves you most. Each can give an insight into a different facet of your life:

1. *Your first choice is known as your "soul bottle" and gives insights into your mission in life.*

2. *Your second choice brings to your attention the challenges you have to face. It also reveals the talents you have at your disposal that can be used to meet and overcome obstacles in your way.*

3. *How far have you come along the way and how have you met challenges? These questions are revealed by your third choice.*

4. *Your final choice opens a window to the future and shows your potential and what could be the outcome of your actions and decisions.*

While the first choice is likely to stay the same, you may find that you change your mind about the fourth bottle when you repeat the exercise. This is because, as you progress through life, your ideas are evolving, your mental and spiritual development is ongoing, and your ideas and perspectives are changing. This is part of the process of "opening out" or becoming aware of your life path. Using the contents of your chosen bottles will help you along the road.

The spirit of Equilibrium

0 royal blue over purple magenta
Spiritual well-being
Linked to the crown chakra, this oil may be rubbed around the hairline. It inspires peace and joy.

1 blue over purple magenta
Physical well-being
Associated with the brow and crown chakras. Rub this in around the ears, neck, and hairline. These colors are emotionally calming.

2 blue over blue
The peace bottle
Linked with the throat chakra. Apply this oil to the neck and throat. The Peace Bottle is linked with concentration and self-expression.

3 blue over green
The heart bottle
Work on the heart chakra. Massage this oil into the chest. Creativity and imagination are enhanced by these colors, which help to release emotions.

4 yellow over gold
The sunlight bottle
Linked with the solar plexus chakra. The glorious colors of this oil cannot but help to raise the spirits. Massage it in around the waist.

5 yellow over red
The sunset bottle
This oil works on the base chakra and is massaged into the lower abdomen area. Its colors are classically stabilizing and energizing.

6 red over red
The energy bottle
Linked with the base chakra, this oil may be applied to the lower trunk and soles of the feet. Red has a vitalizing effect.

7 yellow over green
Garden of Gethsemane
Associated with the chakras of the heart and solar plexus, this is applied around the trunk. The energies of these colors soothe and open the heart to love.

8 yellow over blue
Anubis
These beautiful colors have a balancing and restorative effect. 'Anubis' is linked with the throat, heart, and solar plexus chakras. Massage into the trunk.

9 turquoise over green
Crystal cave
Inspiring awareness of one's true feelings, the colors of this bottle are linked to the heart chakra, and its oil is applied to the chest.

10 green over green
Go hug a tree
These colors of Nature bring vision and put our feelings into perspective. This bottle is associated with the heart chakra and its oil is applied to the chest.

11 clear over pink
A chain of flowers
This delightfully named bottle is linked to all the chakras, and may be massaged all over the body. It is linked to intuition and clarity of thought.

12 clear over blue

Peace in the new eon

This oil works on the throat chakra and is rubbed into the neck. It is associated with peace and with the release of emotional problems.

13 clear over green

Change in the new eon

Linked with the heart chakra, and applied to the chest, this bottle evokes transformational processes and change.

14 clear over gold

Wisdom in the new eon

Associated with the solar plexus, the colors of clear over gold promote inner wisdom. The oil is massaged in around the diaphragm.

15 clear over violet

Healing in the new eon

Linked to the crown chakra, this oil is applied to the head and hairline. The bottle is associated with the release of negative feelings.

16 violet over violet

The violet robe

This oil is associated with the crown chakra. Rub into the hairline. Its violet hue is evocative of realization and acceptance of one's abilities.

17 green over violet

Hope

This bottle is linked to the heart and throat chakras. Apply to the chest. Its colors inspire expansion of mental horizons and promote inner strength.

18 yellow over violet

Turning tide

These colors awaken courage and bring joy to the soul. The oil works on the crown and solar plexus chakras and is applied to the hairline.

19 red over purple

Living in the material world

Physical and spiritual, red, and purple unite to raise vitality. Apply this oil, linked to the base and crown chakras, to the abdomen.

20 blue over pink

Star child

Connected with all the chakras, these colors bring out the openness of the inner child. The oil may be applied to all areas of the body.

21 green over pink

New beginning for love

Associated with both the base and heart chakras, this oil is rubbed into the chest. Green and pink prepare us for new situations and open the heart to love.

22 yellow over pink

Awakening

This bottle is associated with the "awakening" of new confidence and direction. Linked to the solar plexus chakra, it is applied to the chest.

23 rose pink over pink

Love and light

Associated with both the base and crown chakras, this oil is applied to the lower abdomen or around the hairline. Its title needs no further explanation.

24 violet over turquoise
New message

Linked to the heart and crown chakras. Appy to the chest and throat. This oil's vibrant jewel colors facilitate communication and help "spread the message."

25 purple over magenta
Florence Nightingale

Purple and magenta inspire us to overcome difficulties in our lives and link this bottle to the crown chakra. This oil is applied around the hairline.

26 orange over orange
Etheric well-being

The effervescence of dual orange pours out of this bottle, lifting and revitalizing. Linked to the sacral chakra, this oil is applied to the abdomen.

27 red over green
Robin Hood

Red and green help to clear emotional blockages, so this oil is linked to the base and heart chakras. Massage the oil into the trunk of the body.

28 green over red
Maid Marion

A companion to bottle 27, with the same links and action. It, too, is massaged into the trunk.

29 red over blue
Get up and go

Red is here teamed with intellectual blue to bring about balance and harmony. This oil, applied to the trunk, is linked to the base and throat chakras.

30 blue over red
Bringing heaven to earth

Together blue and red help us to shed outdated beliefs. Responding to the base and throat chakras, this oil is applied to the hairline or trunk.

31 green over gold
The fountain

Gold and green are stabilizing colors, which calm and bring inner happiness. Connected with the heart and solar plexus, this oil is applied to the chest.

32 royal blue over gold
Sophia

Royal blue and gold combine to awaken our higher minds. Working on the brow and solar plexus chakras, apply from the head to the waist.

33 royal blue over turquoise
Dolphin

Linked to the brow and heart chakras, this oil may be applied to the hairline. It is associated with self-discovery and creative breakthroughs.

34 pink over turquoise
Birth of Venus

Delicate pink and turquoise gently open the heart to the blossoming of new love. This oil can be applied to the hairline, the chest, or even the lower abdomen.

35 pink over violet
Kindness

For the base and crown chakras, the Kindness oil may be applied all over the body. These colors have a revivifying action, raising low spirits.

36 violet over pink

Charity

Associated with base and crown chakras, this oil is applied to all areas of the body. Together, violet and pink help to neutralize negative thinking.

37 violet over blue

The Guardian Angel comes to Earth

Violet and blue are pathfinders, opening minds to new directions. Linked to the crown and throat chakras, this oil is applied to the hairline or throat.

38 violet over green

Troubadour

These colors help us develop our true potential. Applied to the head, chest, and abdomen, this bottle responds to the heart and crown chakras.

39 violet over gold

The puppeteer

Assisting the chakras of the crown and solar plexus, this oil is applied to the hairline and abdomen. These colors awaken our intuition, empathy, and joy.

40 red over gold

"I am"

Helping the flow of energy through the system. Affiliated to the base and solar plexus chakras, this oil may be massaged into the abdomen.

41 gold over gold

El Dorado

Gold brings happiness to the soul and promotes wisdom by combining logic with intuition. Linked to the solar plexus chakra, apply to the center of the trunk.

42 yellow over yellow

Harvest

Another bottle associated with the solar plexus chakra, this is applied around the diaphragm. Here yellow is the color of communication and clarity.

43 turquoise over turquoise

Creativity

Turquoise works on our creativity center, encouraging us to express ourselves through our talents. Massage this oil, linked to the heart chakra, into the chest.

44 lilac over pale blue

The Guardian Angel

These colors help us to ease past hurts and instill inner peace. This oil works with the throat and crown chakras. Apply to the hairline and neck.

45 turquoise over magenta

Breath of love

A strong color combination which emboldens and strengthens. Linked to the base, heart, and crown chakras, it is applied all over.

46 green over magenta

The wanderer

This fusion of color helps us find new meaning and direction. This oil is linked to the heart and crown chakras. Apply to the chest and lower abdomen.

47 royal blue over lemon

Old soul

Working on the brow, heart, and solar plexus chakras, this oil is applied to the hairline and chest. Soothing and calming, these colors relieve fatigue.

The spirit of Equilibrium

48 violet over clear
Wings of healing
Linked to the crown chakra. Apply this oil around the hairline and abdomen. These colors replace loneliness and emptiness with purpose and hope.

49 turquoise over violet
New messenger
This color combination helps us take change in our stride. Resonating with the heart and crown chakras, apply this oil to the chest, neck, and hairline.

50 pale blue over pale blue
El Morya
A gentle but ethereal color combination which helps us to find forgiveness. This bottle corresponds to the throat chakra and may be applied to the neck.

51 pale yellow over pale yellow
Kuthumi
Stimulating the mind, pale yellow inspires us to temper the intellect with wisdom. This oil is linked with the solar plexus. Apply to the diaphragm area.

52 pale pink over pale pink
Lady Nada
The palest of pinks inspires self acceptance and unconditional love. This bottle is linked to the base and crown chakras. Apply to the abdomen.

53 pale green over pale green
Hilarion
Pale green connects us with spring and hope of new beginnings. This oil, associated with the heart chakra, is applied to the upper chest.

54 clear over clear
Serapis Bay
Assisting all the chakras, this oil is a fundamental aura cleanser and purifier. It can be applied all over the body.

55 clear over red
The Christ
Linked to the base chakra, red has a revitalizing effect. When combined with the clear, it helps us resolve our anger. Massage into the lower abdomen.

56 pale violet over pale violet
Saint Germain
This bottle works on the crown chakra and has a calming and soothing effect when applied around the hairline.

57 pale pink over pale blue
Pallas Athena and Aeolus
Pink corresponds to the base chakra and blue to the throat. Together, they harmonize our instincts and emotions. Apply to the neck and abdomen.

58 pale blue over pale pink
Orion and Angelica
Another base, throat, and crown chakra link, this oil is a great balancer. Apply to abdomen, throat, and hairline.

59 pale yellow over pale pink
Lady Portia
These colors encourage elimination of unwanted thoughts and habits. This bottle is linked with the sacral chakra and is massaged into the abdomen.

60 blue over clear

Lao Tsu and Kwan Yin

With its soothing action, blue/clear frees us to express our innermost feelings. Associated with the throat chakra, apply to the neck and throat.

61 pale pink over pale yellow

Sanat Kumara and Lady Venus

These colors can be a balm for the soul in times of spiritual need. This bottle finds a resonance with the sacral chakra. Massage into the abdomen.

62 pale turquoise over pale turquoise

Maha Chohan

Turquoise prompts us to relax. Associated with the heart and throat chakras, apply to the chest and neck.

63 emerald green over pale green

Djwal Khul and Hilarion

Nature's colors in this combination put us at ease with our own psyche. Linked to the heart chakra. Apply to the chest.

64 emerald green over clear

Djwal Khul

Another oil for the heart chakra, applied to the chest, whose colors evoke the rhythms of Nature. Emerald brings us insights into our feelings.

65 violet over red

Head in Heaven and feet on Earth

Associated with the base and crown chakras, this oil encourages energy flow through the body and is applied to the abdomen and hairline.

66 pale violet over pale pink

The actress

Associated with the base and crown chakras and applied to the abdomen and hairline, these colors inspire us to appreciate the beauties of life.

67 magenta over magenta

Divine love

The contents of this bottle work on all the chakras. It makes a good massage oil for the whole body. This color helps us to focus powers of concentration.

68 blue over violet

Gabriel

Associated with the throat, brow, and crown chakras, this oil may be applied around the hairline and throat. Its colors transport us to wider horizons.

69 magenta over clear

Sounding bell

Another bottle that relates to all the chakras and which may be massaged into all parts of the body. The colors inspire clear perception.

70 yellow over clear

Vision of splendor

The stimulating qualities of yellow fuse with the clear to promote a desire to achieve one's goals. Linked to the solar plexus chakra, apply to the waist.

71 pink over clear

The jewel in the lotus

Since pink describes an inherent sensuality, so this bottle evokes loving tenderness. It resonates with the base chakra. Apply to the lower abdomen.

72 blue over orange
The clown
This combination of colors produces both jollity and insight—the nature of the clown. Massage into the neck, as it vibrates with the chakra of the throat.

73 gold over clear
Chang Tsu
This combination heightens our awareness of our psychological processes. Associated with the solar plexus chakra, apply to the abdomen.

74 pale yellow over pale green
Triumph
Use on the diaphragm and chest. This oil relates to the solar plexus and heart chakras. Its color energies encourage perception and self-acceptance.

75 magenta over turquoise
Go with the flow
A whole–body oil which works with all the chakras. This color combination calms the mind and encourages us to cultivate mellowness in our lives.

76 pink over gold
Trust
Linked to the base and solar plexus chakras, this oil is applied all around the abdomen. This bottle promotes confidence and self-respect.

77 clear over magenta
The cup
An all-over body oil, associated with all the chakras. Its color combination assists the development of mental clarity and brings a sense of perspective.

78 violet over purple magenta
Crown well-being
Associated with the crown chakra, and so applied around the hairline, the depth and richness of these colors help to calm the emotions.

79 orange over violet
Ostrich
Also linked to the crown chakra and rubbed in around the hairline. Violet triggers higher awareness while orange encourages self-love.

80 red over pink
Artemis
This oil is applied to the abdomen, since the bottle is linked to the base chakra. Red and pink work together to bring compassion and understanding.

81 pink over pink
Unconditional love
Pink fosters gentle love within our relationships and acceptance of ourselves and others. This is a base chakra oil. Rub into the abdomen.

82 green over orange
Calypso
Applied to the trunk regions, this oil is linked to the heart chakra. This combination rebalances the system and opens the heart to the joy of the new.

83 turquoise over gold
Open Sesame
Working with the chakras of the heart and solar plexus. Apply to the trunk. Use these colors to help you understand your fears and make choices.

84 pink over red

Candle in the wind

Linked to the base chakra and applied to the abdomen. Helps work through resentment and reach out with love.

85 turquoise over clear

Titania

Encourages us to see potential in new situations and shine our light. Linked to the heart chakra, apply to the chest.

86 clear over turquoise

Oberon

Associated with the heart chakra and applied to the chest. Brings enlightenment and improves communication.

87 coral over coral

The wisdom of love

This oil is linked to the sacral chakra and massaged into the abdomen. Helps with discernment.

88 green over blue

Jade emperor

Linked to the heart and throat chakras, and applied to chest and neck. These colors help rebalance mind and spirit.

89 red over purple magenta

Energy well-being

Works with the base chakra. Apply to the abdomen. Stimulates the grounding energies of the base chakra.

90 gold over purple magenta

Wisdom well-being

Corresponding to all chakras. Apply to the abdomen. This oil brings joy to triumph over our fear.

91 olive over olive

Feminine leadership

Linked to the solar plexus and heart chakras. Apply to the abdomen and chest. Olive strengthens self-belief.

92 coral over olive

Gretel

Linked with heart and throat chakras. Apply to the abdomen and chest. Brings insight and confidence.

93 coral over turquoise

Hansel

Linked to the heart chakra and applied to the trunk. Encourages us to overcome difficulties and independence.

94 pale blue over pale yellow

Archangel Michael

Rub into the chest and abdomen. Linked to the solar plexus, this encourages generosity of spirit.

95 magenta over gold

Archangel Gabriel

Another all over body oil, and associated with all the chakras, this bottle promotes wisdom.

96 royal blue over royal blue

Archangel Raphael

Works with the brow chakra. Apply this oil to the forehead to awaken and inspire the higher mind.

97 gold over royal blue

Archangel Uriel

Linked to the solar plexus and brow. Applying this oil helps to refine our better natures and higher selves.

The power of the pomanders

While the Aura-Soma Equilibrium bottles work on the chakras, the pomanders act on the aura. These holistic oils are not rubbed into the skin. In fact, they do not need to come into contact with the body at all. Unlike the Equilibrium energies, which, once they are absorbed into the skin, work from the inside outward, the pomanders work in reverse—from the outside inward. The action of the pomander essences, though subtle, is no less effective or supportive, because their beneficial influence directly affects the electromagnetic field—or aura—that surrounds our bodies.

We know that emotional problems, fear, tiredness, illness, stress,

The pomander oils interact with our electromagnetic fields and help to shore up our auras. Our instinctive choice of color is often the very one our system needs.

pollution, and the general daily grind can all deplete our energies. This, in turn, results in discoloration or imbalance in our auras. And here is precisely where the Aura-Soma pomanders are useful, for their action helps to shore up our auric fields and strengthens our energies, helping to minimize any damage that may have occurred.

A rainbow of protection

The pomander essences come in a range of colored phials. They may be used in conjunction with the Equilibrium oils or on their own. Each contains the concentrated extracts of herbs and flowers in an alcohol base, which allows the essences to evaporate. Crystal energies and fragrances are also incorporated.

As with the Equilibrium bottles, we are all drawn to one or other of the pomanders at any one time, being attracted principally by its color, which we intuitively recognize as the very color we require to restore our own aura to its full and natural brilliance.

Select your pomander on a daily basis, choosing which instinctively feels right. There are currently fourteen pomanders, with new ones being introduced all the time, but you can work effectively with a range of seven colors.

Once you have made your selection, use your pomander to throw a cloak of protection around yourself if you feel down or jaded. Use it when you require the courage to face a difficult situation, when you need a shield of defense, or want to give your body or soul time and space to recuperate and become whole again.

How to use the pomanders

The pomander oils may be used in several different ways:

To comb your aura

Sprinkle three drops into your left hand, and rub both palms together. Now, run your hands all around your outline, about 3–4 in. (8–10 cm.) away from your actual body, and play your fingers through your aura in the same way as you might stroke or comb your hair. As the oil evaporates, its energies will interact with your electromagnetic field, giving it strength and gloss.

To cleanse the atmosphere

Sprinkle a few drops into your palm and wave your hand around in the room to cleanse the atmosphere or to revitalize and rebalance the energies in your environment.

As massage oils

Although the pomanders are not primarily intended as massage oils, they may be applied to individual acupressure points. Alternatively, once you have dropped some into the palm of your hands, you may simply breathe in their fragrance, allowing their gentle action to take place.

To boost confidence and provide protection

Because the pomanders are contained in small phials, your favorite one can be carried in your bag or pocket and rubbed into your hands inconspicuously at any time you feel you need a boost of confidence or the protection of a "subtle cloak" around you. Alternatively, use it just as you might perfume, for its exquisite fragrance is an integral part of the pomander's restorative potential.

Sprinkling a few drops of colored pomander oil on your palms and breathing in the essence can impart a great sense of well-being.

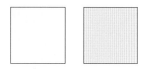

Color as fragrance

The Aura-Soma pomanders come in a stunning range of colors, from white to deep magenta. Choose one to use every day, and discover their individual properties and uses on the following pages.

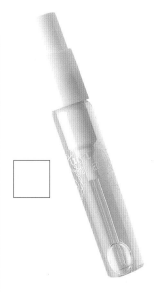

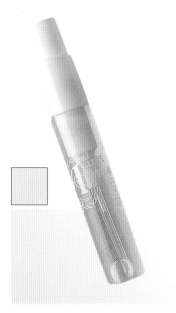

white

Containing kajeput and laurel, quartz and selenite, the white pomander is especially useful to anyone working with computers and word-processors. It is particularly recommended as a general- purpose rebalancer, since white incorporates all the colors of the rainbow in one. Its energies are quintessentially restorative.

pink

Reminiscent of rose petals, the pink pomander has an essentially floral fragrance. It contains rose oil and tourmaline energies and is especially recommended for lovers in the early stages of a new relationship, since it encourages tenderness and affection while protecting the individuals from any emotional hurt. Its action is fundamentally harmonizing.

deep red

With its spicy, cedar scents, this pomander takes us to the forests and reminds us of our roots. No wonder, then, that it has the power to ground us and to bring us back to earth. Garnets and rubies are its crystal energies, and its rich color gives a hint of its energizing potential.

stimulating ∘ balancing

supporting ∘ protecting

revitalizing ∘ energizing

red

The heady, exotic combined fragrance of carnation and sandalwood has a stimulating effect and helps to restore our balance of energy. This is a useful pomander for warding off negative thinking or aggressive feelings, either from ourselves toward other people, or from others directed at us.

stimulating ◦ restoring

orange

Energized with topaz and redolent of the East, this pomander is suffused with the fragrances of cinnamon and mandarin. Its action is one of release, helping us to let go of past memories, trauma, and unhealthy dependencies of any kind. Here the energies of orange invigorate our senses and harmonize the sacral chakra.

energizing ◦ releasing

gold

Amber and mint combine to produce a sharp, fruity fragrance in this pomander, whose golden tones are reminiscent of sunshine. Use it to help you connect with your inner wisdom and to inspire you to recognize the power of simplicity.

balancing ◦ invigorating

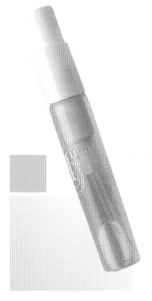

yellow

With essential oils of citronella and infused with the energies of citrine and yellow quartz, this pomander gives off the fresh scent of lemons to awaken the senses. It is of special benefit when we need to strengthen our determination to break bad habits, or when we need encouragement.

awakening
stimulating

olive green

Herb essences, lavender, and pine combine with the energies of jade and adamite to bring us resolve and help us to make sound decisions. The action of the olive green pomander works on our confidence and self-assurance, giving us the courage to know our own minds and to be ourselves.

decisive
encouraging

emerald green

Calming and soothing are the effects of this pomander, with its essential oils of rosemary and crystal energies of emerald and malachite. This pomander helps us to center and balance ourselves, and thereby to see life from a new perspective.

calming
centering

turquoise

Aquamarine and cedar oils contribute to this pomander's sparkling green–blue color and fresh, spicy scent. Especially useful for dissolving creative blocks, it is recommended for all those involved in communications and language work, or who are engaged in the expressive arts.

supporting
strengthening

sapphire blue

The intoxicating fragrance of lily-of-the-valley, coupled with the energies of the blue agate, stimulates inspirational ideas. In addition, this pomander is supportive for those individuals who are psychically sensitive.

inspiring
energizing

royal blue

Use this pomander to heighten the senses, enhance intuition, and stimulate the imagination. Containing blue chamomile and energized with lapis lazuli, the royal blue pomander has a sweet fragrance which instantly brings the heart of the woodland into our souls.

enhancing
supporting

violet

With this pomander we can heighten our awareness and open ourselves to new experiences. Essential oils of violet, rose, and lavender combine with energies of diamond and amethyst to bring us peace and calm, in which to appreciate our blessings and the divine in every single thing.

freeing
calming

deep magenta

Suffused with lavender and frankincense and energized with ruby richness, this pomander encourages the fusion of intuition with rational thought. Use it to raise awareness, to lift the spirits, and to achieve clarity of vision about your path and mission in life.

restorative
strengthening

Your personal colors

The cosmetic effects of color are no less therapeutic than the color techniques that are used in healing—but only if you know how to use colors to your advantage. The most effective way is in the clothes you wear. Wearing the right colors—that is, the colors that really suit you, that complement your complexion, and the color of your hair and eyes—can have a magically transforming effect upon you. The right colors not only will enhance the way you look but can also give you presence, authority, and charisma. Conversely, wearing the wrong colors can make a person look dull, older than they really are, and even unwell. The key lies in recognizing which colors flatter you and which should be avoided at all costs. And for this, you need to find out which color type you are.

Introducing your personal colors

Wearing colors that truly flatter you can make you come alive

Have you noticed how some outfits make you look like a million dollars while others just make you feel dull and insipid? If you have ever stopped to ponder why, you may have concluded that the difference lies in the style, the design, the cut, the tailoring, or the quality of the fabric, perhaps. Certainly all these factors do play a part, but the real reason is perhaps simpler than you think—the color.

The colors you wear can make all the difference to how you look. It does not matter how expensive the price tag, if the color does not suit you, you will neither look good nor feel your best.

Air colors
Colors that are fresh and bright are suitable for Air types.

Projecting an image

The colors you wear also make a statement to the outside world and play a central role in projecting your image. They are how you express yourself, allowing you to silently communicate who you are, what you think about yourself, how you feel, and what intentions you have in mind. Wearing colors that truly flatter you make you come alive; they enhance your personality, get you noticed, and give you personal power and credibility.

So, start to think of the colors you wear as critical factors in your personal image and instrumental in helping you achieve the impact you want to make. Remember, the importance of the way you present yourself to the world can make all the difference. It can ensure that you are the successful candidate at an interview, that you close the deal, that you are noticed by the person you find attractive, or that you are taken seriously when you make a complaint or ask the bank for a loan.

Fire colors
Soft, pastel, or faded colors suit Fire types.

Water colors
Bright, sharp, and vivid colors are best for Water types.

Getting it right

So how do you make colors work for you? It could not be simpler—find the ones that suit you and your coloring and stick to them. Do not be tempted to wear acid green just because it is the color of the season or because it looks terrific on your best friend, or even because your mother bought it for you! If acid green is not your color, it will do nothing for you or for your image.

Finding your colors

For most of us, finding the colors that flatter us best is a process of trial and error. However, that can sometimes take a lifetime, and involve some costly mistakes. Fortunately, there are some shortcuts.

Fashion designers and cosmetic companies recognize that people can be typed according to their natural coloring. Olive skin, brown eyes, and chestnut-colored hair, for example, is one such classification, and quite different from the green eyes, pale complexion, and red hair, that constitute another group. Identifying your personal coloring will show you which of the four main groups (Air, Fire, Earth, or Water) you belong to and give you an instant set of color palettes guaranteed to show you off at your very best.

colors that suit you can:

- *brighten your spirits even if you have not slept for a week*
- *animate your face*
- *put a sparkle in your eyes*
- *minimize your wrinkles*
- *boost your confidence*
- *inspire your thinking*
- *make you look younger*
- *make you feel vital and alive*
- *give you a certain chutzpah*
- *bring you energy*
- *show others what you are capable of*
- *endow you with feelings of personal power*

colors that do not suit you can:

- *make you look tired and washed-out*
- *make you look older than you really are*
- *leech away your confidence*
- *make you feel unhappy*
- *drain you of warmth*
- *rob you of confidence*
- *have a depressing effect on your spirits*
- *make you look harsh*
- *make you appear insignificant*
- *make you look drab and uninteresting*
- *give others the wrong impression of your talents and abilities*

Identifying your color type

The four natural color types each take into account a person's eyes, hair, and skin tone. These are "tonal families" and we each belong to one of the four groups.

Each category is based on physical characteristics, which often bring with them associated personality traits, mental qualities, and health tendencies that are common to that group. Your coloring, it is argued by some people, is the outward manifestation of your inner nature. So, if you have a fiery complexion, you are likely to have a fiery nature. A pale complexion, on the other hand, might suggest someone who is quiet or shy.

The categories

For centuries people have been grouped into four categories according to their colorings and their temperament. These descriptions became known by their elemental associations of Air, Fire, Earth, and Water and are categories that can be used to describe our color families. Today the four groups are sometimes known by the names of the seasons. So Air becomes Spring, Fire becomes Summer, Earth is Fall and Water is Winter. The two sets of names, though, are quite interchangeable.

Air, Fire, Earth, or Water?

To find which group you belong to, start by analyzing your natural coloring. Stand in front of a mirror, preferably in daylight, and take a good look at your skin tone. Regardless of your ethnic origins, your skin will have either a beige/golden/yellow base or a blue/pink undertone. Hair can range from blue-black through auburn to white-blonde. Eyes can go from the deepest brown to the palest gray.

The chart opposite gives a summary of the four categories and shows instantly the colors that suit each type and the colors they should avoid. Use the chart to identify the group you belong to, then turn over to pages 124–131 to find out more.

Putting character to color

Recent psychological studies suggest that there is more than a little truth in the cliché that our coloring reflects our personalities. The color of our hair and eyes, it appears, really does hold clues to our character and behavior—a belief that has been held since the days of antiquity.

Is your hair at the root of your personality?

- *redheads are fiery and prone to mood swings*
- *blondes are bubbly, outgoing, and fun loving*
- *brunettes are studious, sensible, and calm*

Are your eyes the windows of your soul?

- *gray eyes are clever, courageous, controlled, and calculating*
- *blue eyes are sincere, compassionate, self-sufficient, and moody*
- *green eyes are patient, loving, resourceful, and possessive*
- *hazel eyes are imaginative, philosophical, logical, and energetic*
- *brown eyes are practical, serious, committed, but also vivacious*

	air	fire	earth	water
season	spring	summer	fall	winter
basic skin tone	beige golden yellow	pinkish blue	beige golden yellow	pinkish blue
natural hair color	warm blonde	blonde light brown	brunette auburn	dark
eye color	blue green hazel	green blue hazel-gray	brown green	brown hazel green, blue
characteristics	chatty vivacious fun loving	sympathetic refined graceful	caring sociable philosophical	industrious focused selective
colors to suit				
colors to avoid				
famous color types	Princess Diana Goldie Hawn	Marilyn Monroe Grace Kelly	Clint Eastwood Sophia Loren	Elizabeth Taylor Pierce Brosnan

Identifying your color type

The air group

When putting together your basic wardrobe, you should include background staples such as ivory, fawn, dove gray, and French navy. These can be accented with peach, coral, powder blue, and golden yellow. See the color palette below for other color ideas.

Color tip: *avoid maroon and black*

Key character traits associated with this group:

lively, chatty, active, outgoing, spontaneous, persuasive, fun loving, enthusiastic, articulate, charming, funny, versatile, vivacious, strong caring instincts, superficial, sporty, impatient, easily bored

You belong to this group if:

∘ *your coloring could be described as delicate*
∘ *your complexion is fair, ivory, or "peaches and cream"*
∘ *your hair is titian red, auburn, blonde, caramel brown, or golden gray*
∘ *your eyes are light brown, blue, green, or hazel*

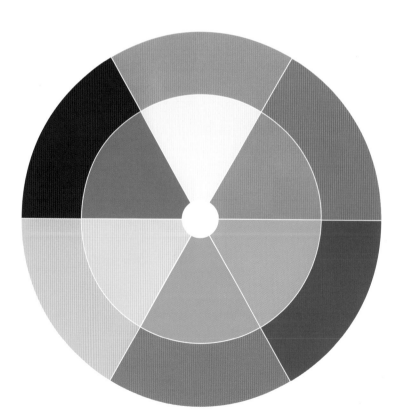

Color profile

Warmth and youthful zest come through the colors typical of the Air group's palette. With their yellow undertones, these colors may be described as clear and bright but without any jarring sharpness.

The fire group

You belong to this group if:

- *your coloring can be described as soft*
- *your complexion is fair, translucent, or has blue or rose undertones*
- *your hair is blonde, light brown, "mousey", or blue-gray*
- *you have freckles*
- *your eyes are blue, green, hazel-gray, or light brown*

When putting together your basic wardrobe, you should include background staples such as camel, clerical gray, navy, pearl-white. These can be accented with rose, pastel blue, or lavender. See the color palette below for other color ideas.

Color tip: *avoid orange, mustard, and black*

Key character traits associated with this group:

well-balanced, tactful, creative, diplomatic, graceful, supportive, artistic, calm, considerate, refined, responsible, sympathetic, consistent, quiet, self-contained, modest, detached, haughty

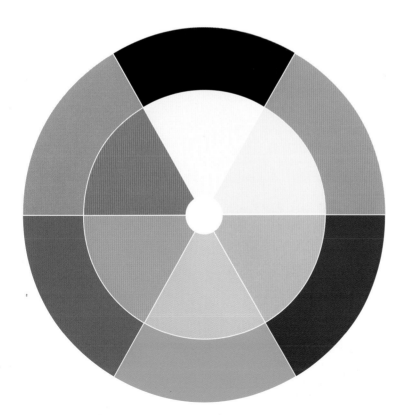

Color profile

Colors for the Fire group are bright but subtle, and even the darker shades have a light quality about them, characterized by undertones of blue or gray. With definitely no dazzle, these colors convey a cool sophistication.

The earth group

You belong to this group if:

- *your coloring can be described as warm and dark*
- *your complexion is peachy, golden, beige, golden-black, or ivory*
- *your hair is brown, chestnut, red, or golden gray*
- *your eyes are brown, hazel, or green*

When putting together your basic wardrobe, you should include background staples such as bitter chocolate, copper, olive green, and pearl. These can be accented with gold, burnt orange, turquoise, and ripe tomato. See the color palette below for other color ideas.

Color tips: *avoid gray, bright pink, navy, mauve, and black*

Key character traits associated with this group:

curious, extroverted, caring, scholarly, sociable, passionate, self-reliant, open, generous, philosophical, analytical, idealistic, honest, helpful, intense, restless, outspoken, critical

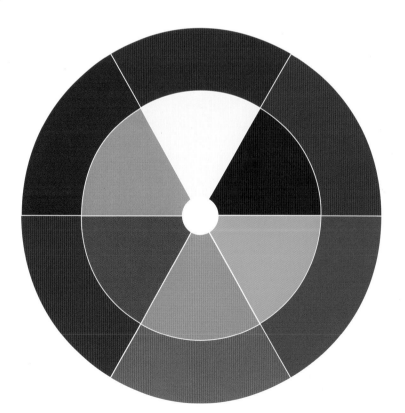

Color profile

Rich, spicy shades fill the palette belonging to the Earth group. Here, colors have an exotic quality, underscored by golden-yellow tones and characterized by a full-blown maturity and depth.

The water group

You belong to this group if:

- *your coloring is strong and striking*
- *your complexion is pale, pink, olive, Oriental, or black*
- *your hair is brown, blue-black, white, or silver-gray*
- *your eyes are brown, hazel, green, or blue*

When putting together your basic wardrobe, you should include background staples such as black, deep navy, charcoal gray, and pure white. These can be accented with red, emerald green, and magenta. See the color palette below for other color ideas.

Color tips: *avoid brown, orange, and mustard*

Key character traits associated with this group:

logical, focused, direct, responsible, cool, confident, hard working, practical, eye for detail, objective, incisive, demanding, pragmatic, selective, achievement-motivated, aloof, status-conscious, emotionally contained

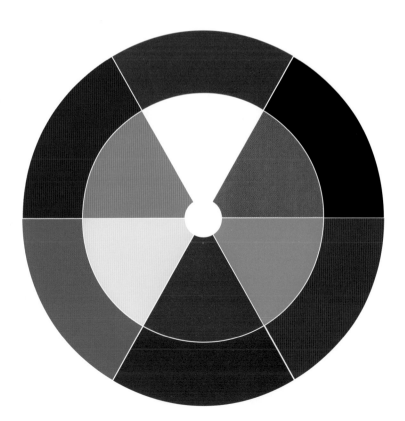

Color profile

Colors belonging to the palette of the Water group crackle with icy sharpness. These colors are pure and unadulterated. With their cool blue undertones, they come across as sharp, punchy, and dramatic.

Getting it right—air

Caramel blond hair, like that shown, places both of these models in the Air category. Colors that are bright but soft, or that have a peachy undertone, as in the off-white jacket worn below, complement their natural coloring beautifully. But notice how the model's looks are drowned by the maroon sweater, and how the brilliant red top throws up the wrong glow, making her look rather florid. When a shirt or blouse is not quite the right shade, tie a scarf in one of the appropriate palette colors next to the face.

colors that suit Air types

Coral, peach, cream, and warm blues make ideal choices for the Air type's wardrobe.

colors that do not suit Air types

Vivid red, murky maroons, black, or stark white, all of which wash out the Air type's delicate coloring, should definitely be avoided.

Getting it right—fire

The word "fire" belies the cool coloring of this type. The color palettes for this category reflect her maturity and sophistication. Her periwinkle blue turtleneck brings out the tones in her skin, hair, and eyes. In contrast, the orange sweater is draining and makes her look tired. If you're unsure whether you're a fire or air type, take the two color palettes to a store with you, and try on a selection of outfits that match each set. You will soon discover which ones bring your face alive and which leave you looking pale and flat.

colors that do not suit Fire types

With their fair complexions and blue undertones, they should avoid peach, orange, and yellow-based colors at all costs, since these work against the delicate tones of the Fire coloring and sallow the skin.

colors that suit Fire types

Muted, faded, and pastel colors suit the complexion and makeup of the Fire individual. Think of delicate roses in an English garden in late summer which have been bleached by the sun, or of dusty lavender, or the pastel pink of seaside rock.

Getting it right—earth

People belonging to the Earth category have a golden undertone to their complexion, so colors that reflect the warm peachy-gold of their skins will be the most flattering. In general, most of the Earthy colors—burnt sienna, paprika, saffron, brick red, ocher, and jade— should suit this type to perfection. Our model is typical of the earth group, and the deep olive green of her sweater precisely complements her coloring, giving her *gravitas* and poise. If you're unconvinced about the colors in your palette, try remnants of fabric in various shades and hold them up to your face.

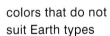

colors that suit Earth types

The Earth palette is characterized by richness and depth and brings to mind the abundance of Nature's harvest. There is no acid sharpness to these colors here, but all is mellow, golden, and sunbaked.

colors that do not suit Earth types

Blue-based colors such as mauve or magenta clash with the golden tones of the Earth complexion. Here, the shocking pink appears almost gaudy against her skin. In the same ways, grays and navys would completely rob her of any warmth and color.

Getting it right—water

With their strong coloring, the members of this category are the only ones who can successfully carry off the dramatic, jewel-bright primary colors of the Water palette. Notice the striking contrast between our model's dark hair and her pale complexion, with its blue undertones, which are set alight by the red of her sweater. And it is only the Water types, too, who can truly look strong and confident in black or white. Compare this to our two models in lime green and gold and notice how these tones bleach out their personalities, making both look pasty and insipid.

colors that suit Water types

This group looks stunning in vivid, blue-based colors such as purple, and magenta and, rather than appearing stark or harsh, black, and white actually give them presence.

colors that do not suit Water types

Creams and beiges; tones that essentially have a yellow base or that take the sharpness out of colors, weaken the impact of the Water type.

Colors of the zodiac

According to astrology, each sign of the zodiac is affiliated to specific colors. Those born under each sign are said to be drawn to, or to express themselves through, their associated hues.

Each sign is also linked to one of the celestial bodies of the solar system whose characteristics are said to represent the nature and disposition of all those born under its dominion. These planets are also associated with a color, which may be added to the attributes of a sign. In addition, signs and planets correspond to minerals and gems, and again, the colors of these stones may also be added to the list.

You can find all your associated colors next to your sign in the chart opposite. Perhaps you are already instinctively attracted to the colors of your sign, so they won't come as a surprise to you. People have an uncanny habit of choosing their sign colors as their favorite colors and of wearing them although unaware of their connections, or even of using them in their home furnishings and décor.

Combining zodiac and personal colors

If you want to be true to your sign and to build your wardrobe around its color, remember to choose its shade according to your personal palette, as described in the section on color types (see pages 118–131). For example, yellow, which is associated with Gemini, ranges from primrose, through citrus, to golden buttercup. If you are a Gemini but belong to the Fire color group, the most flattering yellow for you would be a pale lemon. This shade, however, would do nothing for a Gemini who belongs to the Earth color group. Far better for this person to go for a golden mustard shade, whose warm tones would bring this individual's coloring alive.

So, go for your zodiac colors, but choose your shades with care.

Signs of the zodiac and their associated colors

sign and birthdates	ruling planet	gemstones	associated colors
Aries *March 21—April 20*	Mars	diamond, jasper	
Taurus *April 21—May 21*	Venus	sapphire, emerald	
Gemini *May 22—June 22*	Mercury	agate, jade	
Cancer *June 23—July 23*	Moon	moonstone, pearl	
Leo *July 24—August 23*	Sun	ruby, amber	
Virgo *August 24—September 23*	Mercury	sardonyx, lapis lazuli	
Libra *September 24—October 23*	Venus	chrysolite, rose quartz	
Scorpio *October 24—November 22*	Pluto	opal, beryl	
Sagittarius *November 23—December 21*	Jupiter	topaz, turquoise	
Capricorn *December 22—January 20*	Saturn	garnet, onyx	
Aquarius *January 21—February 19*	Uranus	amethyst, aquamarine	
Pisces *February 20—March 20*	Neptune	bloodstone, peridot	

Color in the future

Natural light
has many
therapeutic
benefits

As color is the visible aspect of sunlight, no work on this subject is complete without taking a broader view of light as a whole and as a source of power and energy in its own right.

Light as a source of healing

The therapeutic benefits of natural light have been recognized by physicians and therapists for hundreds of years. In times past, hospitals and asylums had purpose-built solariums where patients would be placed to absorb the sun's rays, the aim being to speed the healing process. In the nineteenth century, tuberculosis was routinely treated in just this way, exposing patients to pure sunlight in the mountains or by the sea.

In the last twenty years, recognition of winter depression as a medical condition stands as proof of our acknowledgment that sunlight really does

Sunlight has an extraordinary uplifting effect on our systems. When the sun shines, our problems never seem quite so bad.

have a positive therapeutic effect on our well-being. Seasonal Affective Disorder, or SAD, as it is more commonly known, is caused by an overproduction of melatonin, the sleep hormone, which is triggered by the shortening of daylight hours in winter. With this condition, sufferers experience lethargy, a lowering of spirits and feelings of gloom, as their bodies apparently prepare to go into hibernation mode. As energy levels decline, an overwhelming sense of exhaustion and despair descends, and all enthusiasm for living diminishes. Treatment of the disorder, consisting of daily exposure to full-spectrum light, has proved remarkably successful, with sufferers reporting dramatic improvements to their moods and zest for life.

UV light

It is precisely this full-spectrum light and the powerful disinfectant properties of the ultraviolet component of light that are now exciting interest among scientists and medical researchers alike. In laboratory tests, bacteria and other airborne pathogens that have grown resistant to conventional antibiotics have been successfully destroyed with ultraviolet light.

Fighting disease

The use of UV light as an antiseptic is not a new discovery. As in the nineteenth-century treatment of tuberculosis, the potential of light therapy as a curative tool was beginning to find favor among the medical fraternity—and showing good results—only to find its further development curtailed with the introduction of antibiotics. Subsequently research fell into decline.

In recent years, however, the emergence of "superbugs," the reappearance of tuberculosis and the resistance of bacterial infections to antibiotics are forcing us to take a new look at this old form of therapy. Moreover, advances in technology, and, in particular, the use to which lasers can be put, lead us to believe that light therapy is on the verge of a major breakthrough in the treatment of disease, and may be one of the directions that medicine will take in the third millennium.

Light therapy: the treatment of the future

Lasers are used in a variety of corrective surgical procedures

Light therapy—the use of colored rays, fiber optics, and high-powered lasers has revolutionized surgical procedures and medical practices. What might once have been considered imaginative nonsense, straight out of the pages of a science-fiction novel, is now a reality and, furthermore, has been incorporated into mainstream medicine. Lasers, which are essentially intense beams of light, are already routinely used as high-precision scalpels in a variety of corrective surgical procedures, from cosmetic treatments, through ophthalmic (eye) problems, to curing cancers. But even all of this is just the beginning.

Alternative practitioners have long understood the therapeutic benefits of color and light treatments on our health and well-being. Using a variety of techniques, from laying on of hands to color-puncture, healers have claimed that the power of light can cure all manner of ills. Now, many of these claims are being taken seriously, and we are seeing them incorporated into our new technologies, both in the orthodox and complementary fields, with dramatic results.

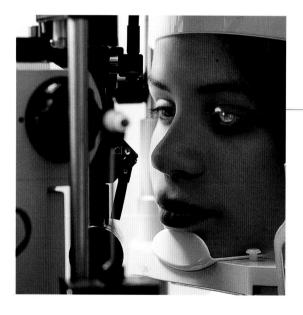

Light has a wide range of applications in the field of medicine, from lasers which become precision cutting instruments, to beams of light in a tonometer which measure pressure in the eye.

Photodynamic therapy

Healing with light and color is the basis of photodynamic therapy, one of the latest powerful tools in the treatment of cancer. Although still in comparatively early stages of development, this is nevertheless an advanced technique which is generating much interest among cancer specialists and offering great promise for the future treatment of a wide range of health conditions.

Described as a relatively painless and non-invasive procedure, photodynamic therapy involves either injecting the patient with a light-sensitive dye for internal tumors or applying it externally in cases of carcinoma of the skin. When the dye is absorbed by the diseased tissue, a powerful red laser beam is used to light up and activate the dye, which destroys the tumor cells—literally at the speed of light—and leaves surrounding healthy tissue unscathed.

Photodynamic therapy, or PDT, has so far proved effective on certain types of cancers, including those affecting the esophagus, pancreas, skin, lungs, neck, and head. With positive results even at this early stage of development, researchers are acknowledging that light treatment has a major role to play in the medicine of the future.

Light relief

Lasers and light boxes able to deliver a selection of powerful color rays have proved successful in the treatment of many dermatological conditions, including acne, eczema, and psoriasis. These systems work by emitting red and blue waves of light, which in turn "excite" and then destroy the bacteria responsible for the condition, and consequently heal the skin. Similar therapy systems, also using colored beams of light, have been successful in the removal of birthmarks, tattoos, warts, moles, and unwanted hair. A growing market, using this technology to smoothe stretchmarks and stem the march of time by reducing wrinkles and other facial lines, is guaranteed to prosper.

Seeing in color

Light therapy treatments have proved especially successful in correcting certain visual and opthalmic problems. The use of spectacles fitted with special colored lenses, for example, have been of particular benefit to people with dyslexia. Epileptics and migraine sufferers, too, reported improvements from similar treatments. And improvements were also noted in cases of certain behavioral problems involving attention deficit disorder, learning difficulties, and poor concentration.

Despite the long history of color and healing, it has required our new technological insights to take another look at light therapy and appreciate its range of applications. Perhaps we are just rediscovering ancient knowledge. Maybe, by standing on the shoulders of giants, we can acknowledge the immensity of the natural and limitless source of energy we have at our fingertips and, with it, truly make a contribution to the future evolution, happiness, and well-being of humankind.

Symbol of a new beginning

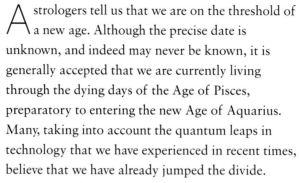

Light is the technology of the future

Astrologers tell us that we are on the threshold of a new age. Although the precise date is unknown, and indeed may never be known, it is generally accepted that we are currently living through the dying days of the Age of Pisces, preparatory to entering the new Age of Aquarius. Many, taking into account the quantum leaps in technology that we have experienced in recent times, believe that we have already jumped the divide.

As a sign of the zodiac, Aquarius represents all that is original and new. It stands for innovation and invention, for advanced concepts and ideas. It is the pioneer, never afraid to experiment, to push forward the boundaries of our knowledge and understanding. Aquarius is synonymous with technological advance, with broadcasting, telecommunications, and reaching out to the masses. Given the rapid spread and up-take of the internet, those who believe that the Age of Aquarius is already upon us may well be right.

Symbolically, Aquarius is represented by two horizontal zigzag lines resembling waves—probably not waves of water, as was thought in centuries past, but more likely to be energy waves in the form of radio, micro, UV, and, of course, visible light, with all its different color frequencies. As we step into the Age of Aquarius, then, one can only wonder at the awesome discoveries that lie ahead—with light as the technology of the future.

In conclusion

Beyond the speed of light

As proof of this evolutionary leap, scientists now claim to have broken through the speed of light —the implications of which stagger the imagination. We have come, in a very short space of time, a long way from Newton and his prism experiments which first explained the color spectrum and the nature of light. His laws of physics have underpinned our understanding of the physical world for some three hundred years. These recent findings, however, which are beginning to suggest that the universe may not be quite as we have been seeing it, are telling us that it might now be time to rewrite the textbook.

Resources

If you would like to find out more about color or healing, the following books are recommended:

Dalichow, I., and Booth, Mike, *Aura-Soma—Healing through Color, Plant and Crystal Energy,* Hay House, 1996

Liberman, Jacob, *Light—Medicine of the Future* Bear & Co., 1991

Ostrom, Joseph, *Understanding Auras,* Aquarian Press, 1987

Palmer, Magda, *The Healing Power of Crystals,* Rider, 1988

Reid, Lori, *Colour Crazy,* Element Books, 1998

Rendel, Peter, *Understanding the Chakras,* Aquarian Press, 1979

Wall, Vicky, *The Miracle of Colour Healing,* Aquarian Press, 1990

Wills, Pauline, *Colour Therapy,* Element Books, 1997

Aura-Soma resources

Aura-Soma captures concentrations of energy. It enhances color with the appropriate herbs, essences, and crystal waveforms, selected for their empathy with each vibration of color. It is a non-invasive, self-selective soul therapy. It takes a holistic approach—clearing and harmonizing the aura and the subtle bodies balancing the electromagnetic field—helping the spirit, the mind, the emotions, and the physical body.

Aura-Soma was started in England in 1983 by Vicky Wall, a pharmacist inspired through prayer and meditation to create a system of well-being through color.

At the heart of the system are the Equilibrium bottles. They are glittering, dual-colored combinations containing the energies of color, plants, and crystals. Vicky Wall felt that Equilibrium was a mirror to the soul, enabling the individual to recognize in their color choices the reflection of their deeper aspects.

The pomanders are designed to give auric protection, acting specifically on the electromagnetic field which closely surrounds the physical body. There are also the quintessences, the subtlest of all the products. These also act on the subtle bodies, but their function is to help us to align ourselves with a particular energy.

Aura-Soma is now available around the world, and the system continues to expand, with new products being introduced all the time. Pages 102–117 of this book are intended as an introduction to this system. It is not advisable to use the poster or book for diagnostic Equilibrium bottle selection, but it is recommended that you contact a qualifed Aura-Soma practitioner. Stockists worldwide are listed below, and they can also be contacted for local registered practitioners. Or visit the official Aura-Soma web site at www.aura-soma.co.uk.

United States

Aura-Soma USA Inc.
American Distributor
Trish or Will Hunter
P.O. Box 1688
Canyon Lake
Texas 78130
Tel: +1 830 935 2355
Fax: +1 830 935 2508
web site: www.aura-soma.com

Canada

Lynn Robinson
2136 Mohawk Avenue
Coquitlam, BC, V3J 6V2
e-mail:
    Balance_4_You@compuserve.com

UK and France

Aura-Soma Products Ltd
South Road
Tetford
Horncastle
Lincolnshire, LN9 6QB
Tel: +44 (0) 1507 533 581
Fax: +44 (0) 1507 533 412
web site: www.aura-soma.co.uk

Belgium

Elizabeth or Krin De Jonge
Apt. 33–34, Chemin des Deux
    Maisons 73
B-1200, Bruxelles
Tel: +32 (0) 2779 3427
Fax: +32 (0) 2772 8597
e-mail:
    aura-soma.belgium.dejonge@sk

Germany

LF-Naturprodukte
Hans Finck
Treenering 105

D-24852 Eggebek

Tel: +49 (0) 4609 91020

Fax: +49 (0) 4609 9102 34

website: www.lfnatur.com

Denmark

Elly Hinz

Kastanievej 13

DK-1876

Frederiksberg C

Tel: +45 (0) 3325 2930

Fax: +45 (0) 3325 2930

Sweden

Christine Dilts

Flygelvaegen 170

S-22472 Lund

Tel: +46 (0) 46 126 663

Fax: +46 (0) 46 126 663

Norway

Aura-Soma Norway

Madhuri Kielland

Sondrevin 17

0378 Oslo

Tel: +47 (0) 22 14 20 25

Fax: +47 (0) 22 14 21 14

e-mail: nor@aura-soma.no

web site: www.aura-soma.no

Austria

Aura-Soma Austria

Hanni Reichlin-Meldegg

Silbergasse

A-1190 Wein

Tel: +43 (0) 1368 8787

Fax: +43 (0) 1368 1968

e-mail: aura-soma.austria@netway.at

Switzerland

Chinta Struebin

Les Auges

CH-1603 Grandvaux

Tel: +41 (0) 21 799 4202

Fax: +41 (0) 21 799 4203

e-mail: rg.keola@iprolink.ch

web site: www.keola.com

Italy

Aura-Soma Italy

Robert Hasinger

3 Via Civitavecchia

Int 7, 00198 Rome

Tel: +39 (0) 6884 1534

Fax: +39 (0) 6853 01829

e-mail: aura-soma@flashnet.it

Spain

Aura-Soma Spain

Pablo Martin Bearne

Moralzarzal 66

28034 Madrid

Tel: +34 (0)1734 7237

Fax: +34 (0)1734 7237

Greece

Anna Maria Critchley

Antinoros 42–44

16121 Kasariani, Athens

Tel: +30 (0) 172 17952

Fax: +30 (0) 172 17952

Australia

Aura-Soma Australia

Harry or Marg Simon

10 Cygnet Place

Illawong, NSW, 2234

Tel: +61 (0) 2 9651 1066

Fax: +61 (0) 2 9543 0240

e-mail: simon@aura-soma.co.au

New Zealand

Aura-Soma New Zealand

Brenda Stanford

13 Carlisle Road

Browns Bay

Auckland

Tel: +64 (0) 9478 1311

Fax: +64 (0) 9478 1312

South Africa

Aura-Soma South Africa

Melissie Jolly

5 St. Mary's Road

Kloof, Durban, 3610

Tel: +27 (0) 31764 5455

Fax: +27 (0) 31764 5455

Index

Acknowledgments

Author's acknowledgments

I am indebted to Dr. Andy Morley and Dr. Tim Auburn for their invaluable help in the chapters on the psychology of color. To Anna Gunning for so generously talking me through the color groups. And especially to Mike Booth and the inspirational beauty of the Aura-Soma Equilibrium bottles and pomanders, whose jeweled colors make me weep with joy.

Picture credits

The publishers would like to thank the following sources for their kind permission to reproduce the pictures in this book:

t=top, *l*=left, *b*=below, *c*=center, *r*=right.

Aura-Soma: 104–109; P. Barton/Stockmarket: 27; Crown Decorative Products Ltd.: 13*c*, 41, 60*b*, 43, 45, 118*b*; E.W.A.: 40, 42, 44; Gina Glover/Photofusion: 134; J. Greim/SPL: 136; David Hanover/Stone: 25; Kim Heacox/ Stone: 6; Aaron Horowitz/Corbis: 31; Garion Hutchings/SPL: 18, 66; Tony Hutchings/Stone: 8; Michael Keller/Stockmarket: 23; John Marshall/Stone: 34; Clive Nichols Garden Pictures: 98; Nicholas Parfitt/Stone: 14; Lori Adamski Peek/Stone: 21; Powerstock-Zefa: 35, 50; Chris Simpson/Stone: 29; David Stewart/Stone: 33; Superstock: 64; V&A Museum, London/Bridgeman Art Library: 63.

All other photographs Claire Paxton.
Illustrations on pages 16, 47, 70, 72–77, 84-87, and 92 by Anthony Duke.

Eddison Sadd would like to thank all the models: Sue Atu, Nicola Dixon, Sarah King, Makiko Parsons, and Lindsey Scott; and Paula Pryke for the loan of the vases used on the front cover.

Eddison•Sadd Editions

Commissioning Editor Liz Wheeler
Editors Sophie Bevan, Nicola Hodgson
Proofreader Ann Kay
Americanization Eleanor Van Zandt
Indexer Dorothy Frame
Art Director Elaine Partington
Art Editor Hayley Cove
Picture Researcher Diana Morris
Make-up Artist Kate Liasis
Production Karyn Claridge, Charles James